KENTUCKY WILDLIFE VIEWING GUIDE

Carolyn Hughes Lynn, Author
Bob Berry, Project Coordinator

FALCON™

Helena, Montana

ACKNOWLEDGMENTS

Kentucky Department of Fish and Wildlife Resources (KDFWR) division directors Lynn Garrison, Public Affairs and Policy (formerly Information and Education director), and Lauren Schaaf, Wildlife, made this viewing guide possible by budgeting for the Kentucky Watchable Wildlife Program and its coordinator.

This book would not have been possible without the talents and valued contributions of the dedicated members of the Kentucky Wildlife Viewing Guide Steering Committee. The committee is composed of Bob Berry, chairman, Carolyn Hughes Lynn, Charlie Logsdon and Danny Watson, KDFWR; Carey Tichenor, Kentucky Department of Parks; Kris Snyder, Kentucky State Nature Preserves Commission; Phyllis Brandon, National Park Service; Bernita "Bernie" McCloud, David Jackson, Bob Beverley and Danny Barrett, U.S. Army Corps of Engineers; Larry Martoglio, U.S. Forest Service; Steve Bloemer, TVA's Land Between the Lakes (LBL); Mike Lorton, Lexington/Fayette County Parks; and Steve Goodwin, Louisville/Jefferson County Metro Parks.

Program coordinator Bob Berry spent many hours traveling Kentucky's highways and byways, evaluating sites and checking accuracy of directions. John Boone, KDFWR, provided valuable assistance by consulting on design. Denise Mangan, KDFWR, eased the writer's job by entering information from site nomination forms on computer disc. Wildlife artist Rick Hill, KDFWR, graciously found time to illustrate Kentucky's birds and animals, grouped by three major regions — East, Central and West. A big thank-you to Elaine Breeck, KDFWR, who proofread and diligently checked copy against nomination forms. Jill Krooper and Steve Bloemer, LBL, also proofread copy.

Special appreciation goes to on-site mangers and others who provided nominations, interviews and tours.

Author
Carolyn Hughes Lynn

Project Coordinator
Bob Berry

Illustrations
Rick Hill

Front Cover Photo
Kentucky warbler STEVE MASLOWSKI

Back Cover Photos
Land Between the Lakes JEFFREY A. BROWN
Raccoon GENE BOAZ

CONTENTS

REGION THREE: NORTH-CENTRAL

REGION FOUR: EASTERN

PROJECT SPONSORS

 KENTUCKY DEPARTMENT OF FISH AND WILDLIFE RESOURCES. The Kentucky Department of Fish and Wildlife Resources is the steward of the commonwealth's natural diversity—its wildlife and habitats. In partnership with people, department personnel will use their collective knowledge and skills to understand and manage these resources to meet the needs and hopes of present and future generations. Kentucky Department of Fish and Wildlife Resources, #1 Game Farm Road, Frankfort, KY 40601; (502) 564-3400.

 KENTUCKY DEPARTMENT OF HIGHWAYS. The mission of the Kentucky Department of Highways is to provide a safe, efficient, environmentally sound and fiscally responsible transportation system which promotes economic growth and enhances the quality of life in Kentucky. Goals include leading the nation in developing and operating quality transportation systems; delivering the best possible service to all customers; integrating sound environmental practices in everything undertaken; and, promoting employee excellence through improved communication, professionalism and career development opportunities. The Kentucky Department of Highways is administered by the Transportation Cabinet. Kentucky Department of Highways, Frankfort, KY 40601; (502) 564-4890.

 KENTUCKY DEPARTMENT OF TRAVEL DEVELOPMENT. The Kentucky Department of Travel Development markets the commonwealth as a tourist destination. The department uses an integrated advertising campaign, produces travel literature and answers requests for Kentucky vacation information to increase the amount of money tourists spend in Kentucky. Tourism dollars increase state and local tax revenues, employment opportunities and personal income for residents, all of which strengthen Kentucky's overall economy. Kentucky Department of Travel Development, Capital Plaza Tower, Suite 2200, 500 Mero Street, Frankfort, KY 40601; (502) 564-4930.

 KENTUCKY DEPARTMENT OF PARKS. The Kentucky Department of Parks provides quality facilities, programs and services at the numerous state and resort parks and historic sites it operates across the commonwealth. Kentucky's parks department strives to protect the historical, cultural and natural-resource values of all parks. Additionally, each individual park supports the efforts of local communities and citizens. Kentucky Department of Parks, Capital Plaza Tower, 10th Floor, Frankfort, KY 40601; toll-free information hotline, 1-800-255-7275.

 KENTUCKY STATE NATURE PRESERVES COMMISSION. The Kentucky State Nature Preserves Commission affords the highest protection of the commonwealth's rich biological diversity by inventorying natural areas, monitoring rare species and preserving those remnants of Kentucky's natural heritage for people. More than 10,000 acres on 31 state nature preserves provide for rare species and habitat protection, scientific research, education and passive recreation. Kentucky State Nature Preserves Commission, 801 Schenkel Lane, Frankfort, KY 40601; (502) 573-2886.

LEXINGTON/FAYETTE COUNTY PARKS. The Division of Parks and Recreation consistently provides programming in the Lexington-Fayette community for all sectors of the population. The division recognizes that taking time to enjoy recreation and leisure activities is part of a balanced lifestyle that is important to health. Providing quality and safe park facilities in all areas of the community is a major goal. The division strives to offer its programs at no cost, or the lowest cost possible, to participants. Lexington/Fayette County Parks, 545 North Upper Street, Lexington, KY 40508; (606) 288-2900.

 LOUISVILLE/JEFFERSON COUNTY METRO PARKS. The mission of Louisville/Jefferson County Parks is to provide environmentally conscious stewardship of Jefferson County's natural areas for recreational, educational and social development while emphasizing protection and preservation of natural resources. Our vision is to promote public awareness of natural resources through quality programs, facilities and recreational opportunities. We will continue the augmentation and protection of natural lands and resources for the citizens of Jefferson County and surrounding areas. Louisville/Jefferson County Metro Parks, P.O. Box 467, Fairdale, KY 40118; (502) 366-5432.

 NATIONAL PARK SERVICE. The National Park Service provides for the public enjoyment of scenery, wildlife and natural and historic objects while helping to ensure that these will exist, unimpaired, for future generations to enjoy. Mammoth Cave National Park, Mammoth Cave, KY 42259; (502) 758-2251.

 TVA'S LAND BETWEEN THE LAKES. Established in 1933, the Tennessee Valley Authority (TVA) is a corporate agency of the federal government and administered by a three-member board of directors appointed by the President and confirmed by the Senate. TVA's primary responsibilities are flood control, navigation and production of electric power. TVA's purposes for Land Between the Lakes are providing outdoor recreation and environmental education. Land Between the Lakes, 100 Van Morgan Drive, Golden Pond, KY 42211-9001; (502) 924-5602.

 U.S. ARMY CORPS OF ENGINEERS. The U.S. Army Corps of Engineers, which manages 17 major reservoirs in Kentucky, is charged with water resource development for flood control, navigation, fish and wildlife enhancement and recreation. Another major responsibility is supporting the nation and its military in engineering and construction needs. Louisville District, U.S. Army Corps of Engineers, P.O. Box 59, Louisville, KY 40201; (502) 582-5736.

 USDA FOREST SERVICE. The U.S. Forest Service, U.S. Department of Agriculture, provides a continuing flow of natural resource goods and services to help meet the nation's needs and contribute to the international community. In Kentucky, the Forest Service manages Daniel Boone National Forest for sustainable multiple use. Daniel Boone National Forest, 100 Vaught Road, Winchester, KY 40391; (606) 745-3100.

Westvāco WESTVACO CORPORATION. Westvaco is a major manufacturer of papers for high-quality graphic reproduction, consumer and industrial packaging and specialty chemicals for a host of industrial and environmental applications. Westvaco manages 1.5 million acres of timberlands in the U.S. and Brazil for multiple use. The corporation shares its forestry management expertise with its neighbors who participate in Westvaco'a Cooperative Forest Management Program. We all share responsibility for conserving natural resources. This is especially true for Westvaco. Healthy forests and clean air and water are good for our business as well as for people and communities. That is why we stress solid environmental performance that often goes beyond government standards and operations that balance the interests of business and nature. Westvaco Corporation, Timberlands Division, P.O. Box 458, Wickliffe, KY 42087; (502) 335-3156.

 DEFENDERS OF WILDLIFE is a national nonprofit organization of more than 80,000 members dedicated to preserving the natural abundance and diversity of wildlife and its habitat. A one-year membership is $20 and includes six issues of *Defenders,* an award-winning conservation magazine, and *Wildlife Advocate,* an activist-oriented newsletter. To join or for further information, write or call Defenders of Wildlife, 1101 14th Street NW, Suite 1400, Washington, DC, 20005, (202) 682-9400.

Design, typesetting, and other prepress work by Falcon Press,
Helena, Montana.

Printed in Korea.
ISBN 1-56044-304-9

Library of Congress Cataloging-in-Publication Data

Lynn, Carolyn Hughes.
    Kentucky wildlife viewing guide / Carolyn Hughes Lynn, author.
        p.   cm. — (The Watchable wildlife series)
        ISBN 1-56044-304-9
        1. Wildlife viewing sites—Kentucky—Guidebooks. 2. Wildlife
    watching–Kentucky–Guidebooks. 3. Kentucky—Guidebooks. I. Title.
    II. Series.
    QL178.L96   1994   94-38073
    591.9769—dc20   CIP

COMMONWEALTH OF KENTUCKY
OFFICE OF THE GOVERNOR

Welcome to Kentucky. Our natural heritage offers outdoor enthusiasts a vast array of wildlife viewing opportunities.

The Bluegrass State is unsurpassed in its diversity of wildlife, plant communities, and terrain. You will see lush flatlands and cypress swamps in the Jackson Purchase, gently rolling fields and farms in central portions of the state, and the Appalachian Mountains in the east. Numerous forested acres, extensive cave systems, miles of navigable waterways, and one of the best state park systems in the nation underscore the uniqueness of the Commonwealth.

The *Kentucky Wildlife Viewing Guide* contains directions to locations where you will have opportunities to view and photograph wildlife, notice plant life, and listen to the sounds of nature. Many sites are barrier-free. Others have interpretive materials available to increase the quality of your outdoor experience.

The Kentucky Department of Fish and Wildlife Resources owns or manages 1.1 million acres of public wildlife lands across this state. Included are more than 70 wildlife management areas. Several are listed in this guide.

Viewing sites are located throughout the state and may be found by using this guide. Look for the special road signs with the binoculars logo, as shown at right.

This guide is the result of the cooperation of many dedicated people, including state, federal, and private agencies. You will be pleased with this informative, entertaining, and educational book. It expresses our commitment to protecting and enhancing Kentucky's wildlife and habitats.

As you travel the Bluegrass State to view wildlife, you will discover what Kentuckians have known for a long time—Kentucky's wildlife resources are even more important today than when this wild land was settled more than two centuries ago.

I wish you enjoyable wildlife viewing experiences and invite you to return to encounter Kentucky's wealth of wildlife.

Sincerely,

Governor Brereton C. Jones

8

INTRODUCTION

Kentucky's diversity is unsurpassed. From cypress swamps and large reservoirs to rolling, rich farmlands and miles of flowing water to forested mountains reaching 4,000 feet, the Bluegrass State holds vastly different ecosystems supporting numerous, varied wildlife and plant communities.

Kentucky has one of the most intricate cave and underground stream systems in the world. Often undetected, unique, rare wildlife such as cave fish, cave crayfish and the federally-listed endangered cave shrimp live here.

The bulk of Kentucky's endangered species are mussels, followed by birds such as the red-cockaded woodpecker and Bachman's and Kirkland's warblers. Virginia big-eared, gray and Indiana bats are also endangered along with Short's goldenrod, Cumberland sandwort and running buffalo clover. Endangerment is a natural process speeded up by human impacts. Most species that become rare require very specific habitat. Interior least terns, for example, nest in depressions on Mississippi River sandbars near the Jackson Purchase. Red-cockaded woodpeckers require old pine trees with decaying heartwood for excavating nests. At last count, 13 of the woodpeckers are living on Daniel Boone National Forest in southern Kentucky—the northernmost portion of their range. Quite literally, these birds are perched on the edge.

Ponder this: *If the beasts and birds abound no more and fish grow scarce on every shore, what chance have you and I, my friend, to meet a different, gladder end?*

—Author unknown

Numerous wildlife such as white-tailed deer, wild turkeys, coyotes, raccoons, skunks, bullfrogs, mice, shrews, salamanders, crows, hawks, owls and many others are abundant across the state. Black bears are returning to abandoned farmlands in eastern forests. Bald eagles are rearing young near large reservoirs in Western Kentucky. Through restoration efforts, ospreys are once again nesting in Kentucky and river otters are swimming in the slow-moving streams of the eastern two-thirds of the state. Peregrine falcons are returning to city release sites.

Kentuckians care about wildlife. We invite you to share our appreciation and enjoyment of wildlife by visiting the viewing sites listed in this guide.

TIPS FOR VIEWING WILDLIFE

Much of the excitement of wildlife viewing stems from the fact that you can never be sure of what you will see. While many species are difficult to view under the best of circumstances, there are several things you can do to greatly increase your chances of seeing wild animals in their natural environment.

Patience is the key to successful wildlife viewing. You must spend enough time in the field. If you arrive at a viewing site expecting to see every species noted in this guide on your first visit, you will surely be disappointed. Review the tips below, and enjoy your time outdoors, regardless of what you see.

Prepare for your outing. Some of the viewing sites in this guide are remote and have no facilities. Review each site account before you visit, checking for warnings about services and road conditions. *ALWAYS CARRY WATER, EVEN IN WINTER.* Dress appropriately for the area, season and the day's weather. Weather conditions in Kentucky can change rapidly and may vary markedly from one day to the next, especially in spring and fall. Always travel with an up-to-date road map. Kentucky's Official Highway Map is free and available by writing Travel, P.O. Box 2011, Frankfort, KY 40602, or call 1-800-225-TRIP. Additionally, detailed maps of many areas featured in this guide may be obtained through the Kentucky Department of Fish and Wildlife Resources, Kentucky Department of Parks, National Park Service, U.S. Army Corps of Engineers, U.S. Forest Service and other site owners.

Visit when animals are active. The first and last hours of daylight are most productive. Early summer evenings can be good for viewing reptiles. In spring and fall, reptiles and amphibians tend to be more active during the warmest period of the day. Many mammals and birds are quite active before or after storms or on cloudy summer days. Songbirds are especially active immediately after a summer rainstorm.

Wildlife viewing is often seasonal. Many species are present only during certain times of year. Waterfowl and shorebirds are best viewed when they migrate through Kentucky in large numbers. Bald eagles may be seen only in certain months. Each site account contains a wealth of information about optimal seasons for viewing selected species. Consult a field guide for additional information, or call the site owner for an update before you visit.

Use field guides. Pocket field guides are essential for positive identification of the many animals named at each viewing site. Guides, which may be purchased from bookstores, are available for virtually every plant and animal found in Kentucky. Field guides can help you prepare for more successful outings because they contain valuable information about where the animals live, what they eat and when they rear young.

Use binoculars or a spotting scope. Viewing aids bridge the distance between you and wild animals. Binoculars come in different sizes such as 7x35, 8x40, 10x50. The first number refers to how large the animal will be magnified compared to the naked eye. A "7x" figure, for example, means an animal appears 7 times larger than its actual size. The second number refers to the diameter of the lens that faces the animal. The larger this number, the greater the amount of light entering the lens—which means better viewing in dim light.

Move slowly and quietly. When you arrive at a viewing site, you can employ several strategies for getting close to wildlife. You can stay in your vehicle and wait for animals to pass by, or you can find a comfortable place, sit down and remain still. You may choose to quietly stalk wildlife; take a few steps, then stop, look and listen. Use your ears to locate birds or the movements of other animals. Walk into the wind if possible, avoiding brittle sticks or leaves. Use trees and vegetation as a blind. Wear dark-colored clothes or camouflage (except during turkey hunting seasons, April and October). Consider using a drop cloth of camouflage netting or portable blind.

Enjoy wildlife at a distance. You can actually harm the wildlife you care about by getting too close. Move away from an animal if it stops feeding and raises its head sharply, appears nervous, stands up suddenly or changes its direction of travel. Causing animals to run or move in winter forces them to use up critical energy reserves needed to survive. Leave your pets at home—they may chase or kill wildlife.

Never touch orphaned or sick animals, especially skunks and raccoons. In Kentucky, skunks and raccoons may carry diseases harmful to humans. Young wild animals that appear to be alone usually have parents waiting nearby. If you believe an animal is injured, sick or abandoned, do not attempt to rescue it. Instead, contact the site owner.

Some wildlife can be dangerous. Maintain a safe distance from black bears, especially sows with cubs; white-tailed deer bucks in fall and bobcats any time of year. Venomous rattlesnakes, copperheads and cottonmouths are active spring through fall. Be alert, and view these animals from a safe distance if you encounter them.

Honor the rights of private landowners. About 95 percent of Kentucky is privately owned. Some sites in this guide feature viewing locations along road-sides adjacent to private lands. Always get permission from the landowner before entering private property.

Honor the rights of other wildlife viewers. Keep voices low. If many people are viewing, please be patient and allow others to enjoy a quality experience. Leave wildlife habitat in better condition than you found it. Pick up any litter and dispose of it properly.

HOW TO USE THIS GUIDE

Kentucky is divided into **four travel regions** (see state map, following page), with each region forming a separate section of this book. Each section opens with a **regional map** and a list of all viewing sites.

Wildlife **viewing sites** are numbered in a consecutive pattern. Each site features a series of **wildlife icons** (see page 14)—these identify wildlife groups most commonly associated with the site, not every class of animal or plant found there. The site **description** provides a brief overview of the habitats and physiographic features found at the site, along with notes on wildlife species. It is followed by a **viewing information** section, which elaborates on wildlife species, optimal viewing times and locations, and notes on access and amenities at the viewing area. Written **directions** are supplied for each site; a **site map** is also provided if that area is more difficult to reach. Always supplement the directions in this guide with an up-to-date road map. *NOTES OF CAUTION REGARDING ROAD CONDITIONS, VIEWING LIMITATIONS OR OTHER IMPORTANT RESTRICTIONS APPEAR IN CAPITAL LETTERS.*

Also listed at the end of each site account is the name of the **site owner**, along with a **phone number** for obtaining additional information. The name of the **closest town** is also included. **Facilities icons** (see page 14) at the bottom of the page provide important information about fees, lodging, camping, and other recreational opportunities at the site.

NOTE: IN THIS GUIDE, THE BARRIER-FREE ICON MEANS THAT PARKING AND SOME PORTION OF THE VIEWING SITE OFFER UNIVERSAL ACCESS.

KENTUCKY
wildlife viewing areas

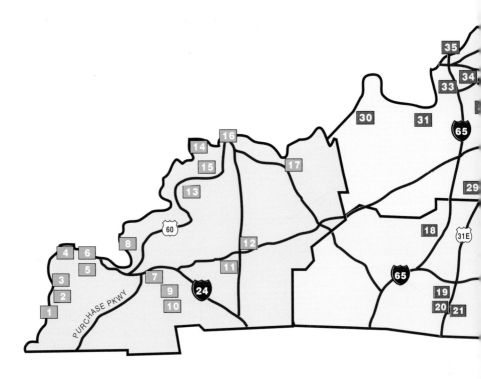

Kentucky is divided into four travel regions, with each region forming a chapter of this guide. Each region appears in a different color on this map. Viewing sites are numbered consecutively.

▢ Region One: Western

▢ Region Two: South-Central

▢ Region Three: North-Central

▢ Region Four: Eastern

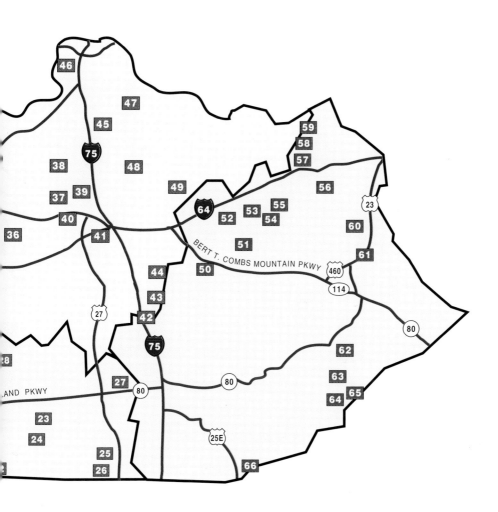

HIGHWAY SIGNS

As you travel in Kentucky and other states, look for these signs on interstates, highways, and other roads. They identify the route to follow to reach wildlife viewing sites.

FEATURED WILDLIFE

 Songbirds Perching Birds

 Waterfowl

 Upland Birds

 Wading Birds

 Shorebirds

 Marine Birds

 Birds of Prey

 Hoofed Mammals

 Carnivores Mammals

 Small Mammals

 Reptiles Anphibians

 Freshwater Mammals

 Seals, Sea Lions, Sea Otters

 Whales Dolphins

 Fish

 Tidepools

 Bats

 Insects

 Wildflowers

FACILITIES AND RECREATION

 Parking

 Entry Fee

 Restrooms

 Handicapped Accessible

 Picnic

 Restaurant

 Lodging

 Camping

 Hiking

 Cross-country Skiing

 Bicycling

 Boat Ramp

 Large Boats

 Small Boats

Icons representing facilities available at viewing locations are listed below directions to each viewing site. As used in this guide, the barrier-free icon means that parking and some portion of the viewing site offers universal access.

WMAs AND HUNTING

Kentucky holds more than 70 wildlife management areas (WMAs). Some are listed in this guide.

From bat houses and nesting boxes for wood ducks and bluebirds to wildflower plots that attract birds and butterflies, WMAs are excellent examples of things people can do to benefit wildlife — from backwoods to backyards. Visitors expecting to view wildlife across manicured expanses will be disappointed. Food plots and agricultural crops left standing in the field are important food sources for birds and animals. Brushy areas, unmowed fields and woods provide both natural foods and places for wildlife to hide. Ponds and watering holes not only provide water for land animals but homes for aquatic and amphibian species.

Most WMAs are open to hunting. Hunting season dates may vary from one wildlife management area to another. Wearing outer garments of hunter orange is also required during certain periods. Before visiting any WMA to view wildlife, check the rules and hunting season dates for the particular area(s) you are interested in. Hunting season information is available from the Kentucky Department of Fish and Wildlife Resources, #1 Game Farm Road, Frankfort, KY 40601; or call (502) 564-4336, M-F, 8 a.m.-4:30 p.m. (Eastern).

REGION ONE: WESTERN

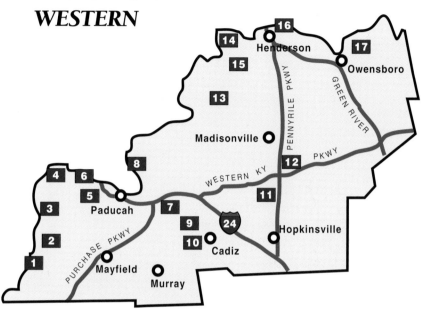

Site 1   Columbus-Belmont State Park
Site 2   Westvaco-Columbus Bottoms WMA
Site 3   Swan Lake WMA
Site 4   Ballard WMA
Site 5   West Kentucky WMA
Site 6   Metropolis Lake State Nature Preserve
Site 7   Kentucky Dam Wildlife Natural Area
Site 8   Birdsville Island - Ohio River Islands WMA
Site 9   Land Between the Lakes
Site 10   Lake Barkley State Resort Park
Site 11   Pennyrile Forest State Resort Park
Site 12   White City WMA
Site 13   Higginson-Henry WMA
Site 14   Sloughs WMA, Sauerheber Refuge Unit
Site 15   Sloughs WMA, Jenny Hole-Highland Creek Unit
Site 16   John James Audubon State Park
Site 17   Daviess Demonstration Area

1. COLUMBUS-BELMONT STATE PARK

Description: Located high on bluffs overlooking the Mississippi River, this park is partially surrounded by a forest of maple, beech, birch, mixed pine, and hardwoods where white-tailed deer and wild turkey are occasionally seen. Look for garter and green snake, lizards, butterflies, and bees during summer.

Viewing Information: Gray squirrel, striped skunk, chipmunk, rabbit, and raccoon are common, as are cardinal, purple martin, and red-headed woodpecker. Self-guided tours; campground; Civil War Museum; snack bar. Fees for museum and camping.

Directions: *From Paducah, take US 62 south to Bardwell, then KY 123 to Columbus and park entrance; from Fulton, take US 51 north to Clinton, then KY 58 west to Columbus and park entrance.*

Ownership: Kentucky Department of Parks (502) 677-2327
Size: 156 acres   **Closest Town:** Columbus

2. WESTVACO-COLUMBUS BOTTOMS WMA

Description: On the Mississippi Flyway, this WMA is managed primarily as habitat for migrating waterfowl, including mallard, wood duck, and Canada goose. Resident species include white-tailed deer, wild turkey, and bobwhite. Bald eagles may be seen during winter.

Viewing Information: *CLOSED NOVEMBER 1 THROUGH MARCH 15;* best viewing June-October. County road through area open year-round except during high water; most roads are gravel and accessible by 2-wheel-drive vehicles. Warm weather brings cormorants, herons, cattle and great egret, red-headed woodpecker, whip-poor-will, and numerous songbirds, including loggerhead shrike. Parking along roadsides. Self-guided drive-through tours, trails, and waterfowl observation areas; slide show and 10-minute video available upon advance request.

Directions: *See map at right. From Bardwell, take KY 123 south for 9.6 miles to CR 1313 (Fish Lake Rd.) turn right (west) and follow signs.*

Ownership: Westvaco Corporation (502) 335-3151
Size: 3,200 acres **Closest Town:** Berkley

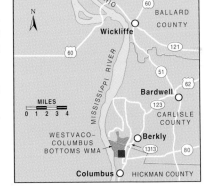

3. SWAN LAKE WMA

Description: Near the confluence of the Ohio and Mississippi rivers, this prime wintering area for migratory waterfowl contains numerous sloughs, oxbow lakes, and Kentucky's largest natural lake, Swan Lake. On the water, look for scaup, pintail, and redhead ducks, along with anhinga. White-tailed deer and bald and golden eagle also present. A bald eagle nest built during the winter of 1988-89 can be seen near Long Pond.

Viewing Information: *CLOSED OCTOBER 15 THROUGH MARCH 15,* but a viewing platform at the front entrance remains open year-round. Interpretive display features area history. In the open season, best viewing is from platform on Swan Lake (follow riprap walkway to lake) and from 4 miles of interior gravel roads. Viewing is best in early morning and late afternoon for deer, waterfowl, and eagles. Other species commonly seen year-round are wild turkey, beaver, muskrat, mink, coyote, red and gray fox, and opossum. In summer look for diamond-banded water snake, painted and snapping turtle, crayfish, groundhog, Indiana and gray bat, killdeer, pileated woodpecker, red-tailed hawk, American kestrel, gulls, dragonflies, and butterflies. Buttonbush and lotus are common in summer. Ten HP boat motors allowed on Swan Lake, trolling motors only on all other lakes; self-guided tours; primitive camping.

Directions: *From Wickliffe, travel US 51/60 west 2.7 miles to entrance sign on south side of WMA.*

Ownership: Kentucky Department of Fish and Wildlife Resources (502) 224-2244 or (502) 564-4406
Size: 2,536 acres   **Closest Town:** Wickliffe

Smallest of all falcons, the American kestrel often appears suspended in mid-air, hovering over highways searching for prey. Feeding on small birds, mammals, and insects, this cavity nester lives in fields, pastures, and suburban parks and yards. Males are blue-gray; females display a rusty color.
GENE BOAZ

17

Description: This prime wintering area for migratory waterfowl and bald eagles consists of bottomland hardwoods, sloughs, and 11 oxbow lakes. Blue, snow, and Canada goose, mallard, wood duck, pintail, northern shoveler, merganser, American coot, and grebes as well as cormorant, anhinga, heron, and egret frequent the area.

Viewing Information: *CLOSED OCTOBER 15 THROUGH MARCH 15,* but a barrier-free observation platform with interpretive display and elevated wetland walkway are open year-round. Sandhill crane and whistling swan are sometimes seen in winter. White-tailed deer, wild turkey, gray and fox squirrel, coyote, red and gray fox, opossum, beaver, mink, and muskrat are frequently seen year-round. Diamond-banded water snake, snapping and painted turtle, crayfish, groundhog, Indiana and gray bat, killdeer, red-tailed hawk, American kestrel, pileated woodpecker, kite, plovers, gulls, and insects are common during summer. Cottonmouth snake rarely seen—best chances during summer. Summer and fall are best for seeing barred and great horned owl, striped skunk, and raccoon. Look for bald and golden eagle in summer, fall, and winter; eastern cottontail rabbit and woodcock in spring and fall. Swamp rabbit, river otter, and bobcat are year-round residents but are rarely seen. Numerous migratory songbirds use the area, including Kentucky warbler, warbling vireo, and scarlet tanager. Common summer plants are buttonbush, lotus, and fire pink. *SEASONAL BARRIER-FREE PIER ON SHELBY LAKE.*

Directions: *See map at right. From Paducah, travel US 60 west 17 miles to LaCenter; take KY 358 for 5.6 miles to KY 473 into Bandana. Take KY 1105 for 6 miles to KY 473; turn left at Lodge Rd., travel 1 mile to area entrance. The gravel road is a 2.5- mile loop.*

Ownership: Kentucky Department of Fish and Wildlife Resources (502) 224-2244

Size: 8,373 acres   **Closest Town:** Oscar

5. WEST KENTUCKY WMA

Description: A mixture of bottomland and upland forests, remnant prairie, and crop and brush land here supports substantial populations of white-tailed deer, wild turkey, bobwhite, woodcock, eastern cottontail and swamp rabbit, gray and fox squirrel, and numerous other small mammals. Seven species of bat and 120 species of songbirds are here, including the brown thrasher and common yellowthroat. The area also contains marshland, warm-water streams, ponds, and some virgin forest, and is possibly the best place in the state to see native prairie grasses. Compass plant, false indigo, blazing star, and black-eyed susan are most brilliant in summer. Fall plants include Indian grass and big and little bluestem.

Viewing Information: Best viewing is from 31 miles of maintained roads. A pamphlet accompanies the drive-through tour. When stopping, pull vehicles to road's edge. Trout lily and recurved trillium brighten bottomlands in spring. In summer look for Indian pink and spiderwort. Depending on river and wetland conditions, visitors may see wood duck, killdeer, snipe, and sandpipers during warm weather. Also watch for great blue heron, American coot, great and common egret, rail, and several species of hawk and owl. In winter look for bald eagle, mallard, and ring-billed gull. Beaver and muskrat are common, as are weasel, river otter, mink, snapping turtle, slider, soft-shell turtle, and racer and rat snake. Guided tours by appointment; self-guided tours; primitive camping. *AREA OPEN TO HUNTING; CHECK SEASON DATES. DO NOT STOP ALONG OGDEN LANDING, DYKES, AND PLANT ACCESS ROADS; THESE ROADS ARE HEAVILY TRAVELED.*

Directions: *See map at right. From junction of I-24 and US 60 in Paducah, travel west 7 miles on US 60. At Future City, turn right (north) on KY 996 and continue 3.6 miles, turn left (west) on KY 358, and travel 2.6 miles to WMA office.*

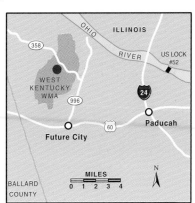

Ownership: Kentucky Department of Fish and Wildlife Resources (502) 488-3233

Size: 6,969 acres

Closest Town: Grahamville

6. METROPOLIS LAKE STATE NATURE PRESERVE

Description: This 50-acre floodplain lake, ringed by bald cypress and swamp tupelo, is surrounded by bottomland hardwood forest. Look for white-tailed deer, wild turkey, and migratory songbirds, including prothonotary and other warblers. Also watch for great blue heron, osprey, and mallard on the lake. Beaver, river otter, raccoon, skunk, and water snake also live here.

Viewing Information: Open sunrise to sunset. Best viewing, is from the 0.75-mile interpretive trail through uplands to lake, early mornings in spring and fall. Birding is good from the parking lot; watch for wild turkey here in fall. Boaters may see waterfowl, great blue heron, and map turtle. *NO GASOLINE MOTORS OR SWIMMING.* Self-guided tours; unimproved area for launching small boats/canoes. *GRAVEL ROADS HAVE RUTS, POTHOLES.*

Directions: From the junction of I-24 and US 60 in Paducah, drive west 7 miles on US 60, then right on KY 996 for 5.9 miles. Turn right onto gravel road, drive past gate to lake parking area.

Ownership: Kentucky State Nature Preserves Commission (502) 573-2886
Size: 123 acres **Closest Town:** Heath

7. KENTUCKY DAM STATE NONGAME WILDLIFE NATURAL AREA

Description: This area provides wintering habitat for up to 50,000 gulls from the Great Lakes, Canadian Arctic, and Prairie Provinces. Kentucky Lake and nearby Lake Barkley host one of the largest concentrations of gulls in the eastern United States, including eleven gull species, some of them regionally rare. Mallard and black-crowned night heron also present. Wading birds and waterfowl are present year-round; gulls and waterfowl peak in winter. Gulls are active daily, feeding on fish below the dam.

Viewing Information: Ring-billed gull is common spring and winter. Herring gull arrives in late winter; Bonaparte's in spring. In winter, Thayer's and glaucous gulls are common; also watch for rarer birds such as great and lesser black-backed, Franklin's, laughing, and California gull, and black-legged Kittiwake. Ducks, heron, sandpiper, killdeer, and barn swallow also visit. Best viewing is from parking lots below dam. Viewing platforms/towers; visitor center open April-November.

Directions: From I-24, drive 2 miles south on KY 453, then west 1 mile on KY 62/641. Signs at dam lead to viewing sites and visitor center.

Ownership: Tennessee Valley Authority (502) 362-4318 or (502) 924-1230
Size: 250 acres **Closest Town:** Grand Rivers

8. BIRDSVILLE ISLAND - OHIO RIVER ISLANDS WMA

Description: From the Ohio River shore, visitors can view large flocks of wintering ducks and Canada geese on Birdsville Island: mallard, black duck, wood duck, American wigeon, teal, gadwall, scaup, and ring-necked duck. Cormorant are also common. The birds find the island's blend of natural foods, planted grains, timber, and sloughs very inviting.

Viewing Information: Best viewing is from mid-October to mid-March. Waterfowl are seen anytime during the day but are most active during first hour of daylight. A paved road leads to barrier-free viewing site.

Directions: *From Smithland, travel east on US 60 for 3.4 miles, turn left on KY 137 and go 3.3 miles to viewing area on left.*

Ownership: U.S. Army Corps of Engineers; managed by Kentucky Department of Fish and Wildlife Resources (502) 753-6913
Size: 390 acres   **Closest Town:** Smithland

Watching wildlife is quickly becoming one of the most popular outdoor activities for all ages in the U.S. The majority of Kentuckians reflect this trend. Involving people in conservation efforts is a major goal of the National Watchable Wildlife Program.
JEFFREY A. BROWN

WESTERN KENTUCKY

BALD CYPRESS

BALD EAGLE

SWEET GUM

SWAMP RABBIT

WOOD DUCK

WATER BOATMAN

AMERICAN LOTUS

GOLDEN SHINER

SMOOTH SOFTSHELL TURTLE

Rich with abundant wildlife, Western Kentucky is the place where the Ohio, Mississippi, Cumberland and Tennessee rivers merge. These river systems and their associated river sloughs, open water marshes, cypress swamps, bottomland forests and adjacent upland farmlands and forests provide some of the most productive wildlife habitat in the state.

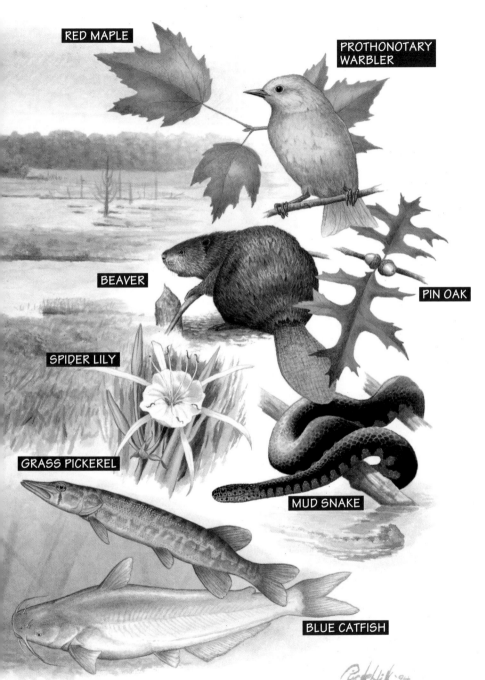

RED MAPLE

PROTHONOTARY WARBLER

BEAVER

PIN OAK

SPIDER LILY

GRASS PICKEREL

MUD SNAKE

BLUE CATFISH

The western wetlands are particularly important for both wildlife and a healthy environment. While providing living quarters for a wide diversity of wildlife species, wetland systems store flood water, trap sediment and filter water, making it clean for all of us.

Description: Land Between the Lakes (LBL), an International Biosphere Reserve, is a 170,000-acre recreation area offering an exceptional variety and abundance of wildlife. Predominantly upland oak-hickory communities support 53 species of mammals, ranging from the tiny least shrew to the American bison (buffalo). More than 230 species of birds visit LBL throughout the year. Upland birds such as bobwhite, wild turkey, and woodcock live here year-round. LBL's 300 miles of undeveloped lake shoreline provides habitat for Canada goose, goldeneye, and bufflehead, green and great blue heron, killdeer and other shorebirds, and one of the largest concentration of wintering and nesting bald eagles in Kentucky. LBL hosts Kentucky's only herd of European fallow deer. A pair of federally-listed endangered red wolves may be seen at Woodlands Nature Center along with other native wildlife.

Viewing Information: Maps, brochures, and directions to best viewing sites available at LBL visitor center and welcome stations. Wildlife may be viewed any time of year, but visitors can check brochures to see when viewing is best for particular species. Excellent viewing from extensive hiking trail system and paved/gravel roads. Trails range from barrier-free to rugged. Interpretive center; blinds, platforms, and towers; guided/self-guided tours. *USE CAUTION DURING TICK SEASON AND SPRING/FALL HUNTING SEASONS.*

Directions: *From I-24, travel 5 miles south on KY 453 through Grand Rivers to north entrance. To east entrance from I-24, travel 24 miles west on US 68/KY 80 through Cadiz.*

Ownership: Tennessee Valley Authority (502) 924-1213
Size: 106,458 acres in Kentucky   **Closest Town:** Canton

Eight years of bald eagle restoration on Land Between The Lakes helped to change the bird's status from federally endangered to threatened in the Southeast (and most of the U.S.) in 1994. Today the osprey, river otter, wild turkey, and white-tailed deer are more numerous in Kentucky than at any other time during the twentieth century, thanks to restoration efforts.

10. LAKE BARKLEY STATE RESORT PARK

Description: Primarily lakeshore forest with numerous woodlots and open areas, this park provides visitors frequent opportunities to view various mammals and bird species. Upland oak, hickory, mixed pine, hardwoods, bottomland hardwood forest, snags, cliffs, cool- and warm-water streams, rock outcrops and dead/down wood are special features.

Viewing Information: Most viewing areas are adjacent to paved roads. All seasons provide opportunities to see a variety of mammals and waterfowl. Best viewing is early to mid-morning and early evening to sunset. Frequently, late-night outings reveal much wildlife activity, especially for raccoons, striped skunks, bats and great horned, screech, and barred owls. Bobwhite, wild turkey, and woodcock are more evident in spring. Ducks and snow geese visit in winter. Grebes, loons, great blue and green herons, egrets, rails, sandpipers, killdeer, gulls, eagles, hawks, falcons, harriers, vultures, kites and osprey may also be seen. Other species that frequent the area are the groundhog, chipmunk, squirrel, rabbit, opossum, beaver, muskrat, mink, white-tailed deer, coyote, fox and bobcat. The harmless hognose snake, that likes to play dead when threatened, is frequently seen spring through fall. Other snakes are the black king snake, black rat snake, northern black racer and northern copperhead. Full-time recreation supervisor, natural history programs year-round; self-guided tours.

Directions: *From Cadiz, travel KY 68 west for 9 miles to park entrance sign and turn right into park grounds; Barkley Lodge sign is 3.5 miles from front entrance. (KY 1489 is 1.6 miles from lodge.)*

Ownership: Kentucky Department of Parks (502) 924-1131
Size: 3,600 acres   **Closest Town:** Cadiz

The nonvenomous eastern hognose snake specializes in eating toads. A pair of large teeth at the rear of its mouth are used to puncture and deflate prey. When alarmed, the hognose hisses, flattens its neck, and puffs up its body to appear larger.
GENE BOAZ

11. PENNYRILE FOREST STATE RESORT PARK

Description: Surrounded by 15,331 forested acres sculpted with cliffs and rock outcrops, this site is home to white-tailed deer, eastern cottontail rabbit, and squirrel. Habitats also include swamp forest with a small grove of bald cypress and a 56-acre lake with bluegill, catfish, crappie, and largemouth bass.

Viewing Information: Best viewing is along entrance drive and behind lodge. Brochures on the park's songbirds, plants, and wildflowers are available at lodge. Look for mallard, wood duck, great blue heron, bobwhite, wild turkey, red-tailed hawk, turkey vulture, and barred owl year-round. Snapping and box turtle are seen in summer. Guided/self-guided tours.

Directions: From the junction of US 62 and KY 109 in Dawson Springs, drive south 6.8 miles on KY 109 to park entrance.

Ownership: Kentucky Department of Parks (502) 797-3421
Size: 863 acres   **Closest Town:** Dawson Springs

12. WHITE CITY WMA

Description: This old surface-mined tract, reclaimed mostly by nature, has a large wetland along Flat Creek, popular with Canada geese, ringneck ducks, and other water birds. Rugged terrain with bottomland hardwoods and upland oak-hickory-pine forest supports white-tailed deer, raccoon, wild turkey, rabbit, bobwhite, and many wood ducks.

Viewing Information: Gravel roads crisscross this site, but walking is the best way to see wildlife. Deer and turkey are often seen crossing roads or in fields. Also watch for rough-legged hawk, northern harrier, turkey vulture, osprey, and kingbird. Beaver, muskrat, mink, coyote, fox, bobcat, weasel, dragonflies, butterflies, mussels, and crayfish also live here. Brown-eyed susans bloom in bottomland hardwoods.

Directions: See map at right. From Pennyrile Parkway, take Mortons Gap exit. Drive east 3 miles on KY 813 to gravel entrance road. Continue 1.4 miles to site.

Ownership: Kentucky Department of Fish and Wildlife Resources (502) 547-6856
Size: 5,472 acres
Closest Town: Mortons Gap

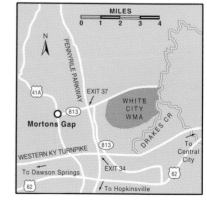

13. HIGGINSON-HENRY WMA

Description: Fields of grasses, food plots, second-growth forest, moist-soil fields, and thickets support bobwhite, ruffed grouse, and wild turkey. Special habitat features are bottomland hardwood forest, snags and downed wood, and mudflats. Upland oak-hickory forest also contains maple, walnut, and birch. A 25-acre lake attracts northern shoveler, green-winged teal, blue and snow goose, grebes, and herons. Marshes and a pond provide food and cover for various aquatic animals and birds such as killdeer and common snipe.

Viewing Information: Songbirds, small mammals, birds of prey, and white-tailed deer may be viewed in and around old fields and forests. Look for reptiles and amphibians spring through fall. Spring is best for viewing songbirds, shorebirds, wild turkey, white-tailed deer, wood duck, and groundhog. In summer look for turkey vulture, summer tanager, and various warblers. Fall brings chances to see red-tailed hawk, northern harrier, owls, osprey, gray and fox squirrel, coyote, red fox, and with luck, gray fox. Bobwhite, doves, and songbirds may be seen in winter along with an occasional bald eagle and woodcock. Also look for switch grass, big and little bluestem, Indian grass, and sideoats grama. Viewing area is on tract 6. Barrier-free viewing platform overlooks lake; camera blind (not barrier-free); 1 trail; self-guided tours. Restrooms at Lake Mauzy camping/picnic area. *OPEN TO HUNTING; CHECK SEASON DATES.* Gas and snacks at Country Corner store, 1 mile from site at intersection of KY 141 and KY 56.

Directions: *From Morganfield, drive east about 6.5 miles on KY 56 to gravel road on left (north) side of highway. Watch for signs and follow to viewing site.*

Ownership: Kentucky Department of Fish and Wildlife Resources (502) 398-3580
Size: 5,424 acres   **Closest Town:** Morganfield

A decade (1980-90) devoted to restoring the osprey continues to pay off, as escalating numbers of the birds return to build nests and raise offspring. Commonly called "fish hawk," the osprey feeds exclusively on live fish snatched from water with sharp talons.

Description: Sauerheber is well-known for hosting large populations of migrant waterfowl during winter. Agricultural bottomlands and managed wetlands regularly attract 30,000 Canada geese and 15,000 ducks of various species. Eagles, hawks, and shorebirds also frequent the area.

Viewing Information: Even though this unit is *CLOSED FROM OCTOBER 15 THROUGH MARCH 15*, observation towers allow views of much of the refuge year-round. Best viewing is along KY 268 between miles 3.5 and 6.5 northwest of Geneva. Best times are early morning to mid-afternoon, November through February. Species seen here include mallard, black duck, green-winged and blue-winged teal, gadwall, American wigeon, ring-necked duck, merganser, tundra swan, and Canada, snow, and blue goose. During fall and winter watch for common snipe, woodcock, cormorant, killdeer, American coot, stilt, great blue and green heron, dunlin, avocet, grebes, common loon, egrets, rails, plovers, sandpipers, and yellowlegs. White-tailed deer are more visible than the raccoon, opossum, and swamp rabbit that live here year-round. Snapping turtle, northern banded water snake, and copper-bellied water snake are on the area in summer but are not easily detected. In summer and fall look for primrose, cattails, and rushes. Paved roads; unlimited gravel parking.

Directions: *Located about 10 miles west of Henderson on KY 268. From Henderson take US 60 west of Henderson to KY 136, turn west, and travel 2.8 miles to junction with KY 268. Drive 4 miles northwest on KY 268 to site.*

Ownership: Kentucky Department of Fish and
Wildlife Resources (502) 827-2673
Size: 3,000 acres   **Closest Town:** Henderson

April and September are the best months for viewing great blue herons along larger lakes and rivers in the western and central portions of Kentucky. The state's heron populations increased significantly following a federal ban on the pesticide DDT.
GENE BOAZ

WESTERN

Description: Extensive stands of bottomland hardwoods with many shallow sloughs and low ridges provide homes for songbirds, wood duck, white-tailed deer, squirrel, and many other small mammals. Two wetland developments allow water levels to be managed on 127 acres adjacent to KY 1629 through the central portion of the unit. *BE PREPARED FOR WET AND MUDDY CONDITIONS.*

Viewing Information: *AREA SUBJECT TO FLOODING FROM THE OHIO RIVER AND MAY BE IMPASSABLE; 4X4 REQUIRED DURING WINTER.* Best viewing during summer, fall, and winter from gravel interior roads and through woodlands (no trail). Hawks, owls, and harrier are common year-round along with raccoon, swamp rabbit, beaver, and muskrat. Warm months bring American coot, pileated woodpecker, great blue heron, great egret, rails, dragonflies, butterflies, and crayfish. Look for snapping turtle, northern water snake, and copper-bellied water snake in spring and summer. In fall and winter look for wood duck, mallard, and teal. Unlimited parking along roadsides; self-guided tours; canoe launch.

Directions: *From Uniontown, take KY 360 east 3.1 miles to KY 1637. Turn left (north) on KY 1637 and continue approximately 1.5 miles to gravel road marked with directional sign.*

Ownership: Kentucky Department of Fish and Wildlife Resources (502) 827-2673
Size: 4,700 acres   **Closest Town:** Uniontown

The great horned owl usually roosts in evergreens and can turn its head 180 degrees. Widespread except in the inner Bluegrass, great horned owls nest in February, choosing abandoned crow or hawk nests in hollow trees to produce 2-3 offspring.
GENE BOAZ

16. JOHN JAMES AUDUBON STATE PARK

Description: On the Mississippi Flyway and known for its migratory birds and spring wildflowers, a portion of this park is dedicated as a state nature preserve. This wildlife oasis within an urban setting features maple-beech forest and 2 small ponds.

Viewing Information: The park is home to white-tailed deer, raccoon, striped skunk, red fox, opossum, great horned owl, Carolina wren and other songbirds, 7 woodpecker species (including pileated and red-headed), squirrel, and rabbit. Also visible are mallard, and great blue and green heron. Little brown bat may be seen at dusk during warm months. Kingfisher and beaver are common at dusk at Wilderness Lake. Year-round bird viewing is available at Audubon Museum-Interpretive Center (fee), with an observation area and hands-on exhibits. *PARK IS CROWDED IN EARLY SPRING, HOLIDAY WEEKENDS, AND FIRST WEEKEND IN OCTOBER.* Full-time naturalist; beach; paddleboats; picnic shelters. Bicycles allowed on paved roads only. Dogs must be leashed and are not allowed in nature preserve area.

Directions: *The park is located on US 41 south of Twin Bridges in Henderson.*

Ownership: Kentucky Department of Parks (502) 826-2247
Size: 692 acres   **Closest Town:** Henderson

17. DAVIESS DEMONSTRATION AREA

Description: This living example of appropriate habitat supporting wildlife consists mostly of open fields with a small pond, wetland area, and native prairie wildflowers and grasses.

Viewing Information: Signs guide visitors on walking tours of this area bordering Pup Creek. Bobwhite, wood duck, American goldfinch, eastern meadowlark, hawks, rabbit, and white-tailed deer frequent the area. Near water look for beaver, mink, muskrat, great blue heron, and various shorebirds. Wildflower viewing is best in spring—look for coreopsis and black-eyed susan. Paved entrance road leads to small parking lot; foot traffic only beyond this point; no other facilities.

Directions: *Area lies east of Owensboro on US 60 and 6.1 miles from US 60 Bypass. Entrance is on south side of road and marked by a sign.*

Ownership: Kentucky Department of Fish and
Wildlife Resources (502) 273-3569
Size: 70 acres   **Closest Town:** Owensboro

REGION TWO: SOUTH-CENTRAL

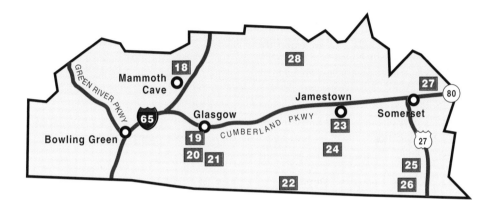

Site 18 Mammoth Cave National Park
Site 19 Quarry Road Watchable Wildlife Area
Site 20 Barren River Lake State Resort Park
Site 21 Dry Creek Unit, Barren River Lake WMA
Site 22 Dale Hollow Lake State Park
Site 23 Lake Cumberland State Resort Park
Site 24 Wolf Creek National Fish Hatchery
Site 25 Cumberland Falls State Resort Park
Site 26 Big South Fork National River & Recreation Area
Site 27 Wesly Bend Unit, Lake Cumberland Marsh Project
Site 28 Green River Lake WMA

18. MAMMOTH CAVE NATIONAL PARK

Description: An exemplar of Kentucky's extensive subterranean landscape, historic Mammoth Cave National Park is an International Biosphere Reserve and World Heritage Site. More than 345 miles of passageways in classic karst terrain make Mammoth the longest cave in the world. Above ground are the rare buffalo clover and a 307-acre remnant of old-growth forest. A wide array of aquatic life thrives in the Green and Nolin rivers.

Viewing Information: White-tailed deer, wild turkey, raccoon, and squirrel abound along rivers and park roadways. Or hike any of the 70 miles of trails to see barred owl, wood peewee, whip-poor-will, wood thrush, eastern phoebe, blue jay, scarlet tanager, and cardinal. Woodpeckers and chickadees are common year-round. Spring and summer, look for great blue heron and belted kingfisher along rivers; warblers (including blue-winged and bay-breasted) along Heritage Trail; black duck, mallard, and beaver at First Creek Lake; wildflowers at Cedar Sink Trail; and deer, muskrat, snakes, turtles, and frogs at Sloans Crossing Pond. On roads, watch for cars stopping to view animals. Cave tours; ranger-led hikes and activities.

Directions: From I-65 South, take exit 53 at Cave City, turn right, and drive 11 miles west on KY 70 to visitor center. From I-65 North, take exit 48 at Park City, turn left, and drive 10 miles west on KY 255 to visitor center.

Ownership: National Park Service (502) 758-2328
Size: 52,830 acres   **Closest Town:** Park City

19. QUARRY ROAD WATCHABLE WILDLIFE AREA

Description: This site features white oaks, a small pond, grain fields, and plots of sunflower, passion flower, black-eyed susan, soybeans, and millet. These habitats are home to white-tailed deer, fox, wild turkey, bobwhite, eastern cottontail rabbit, red and grey squirrel, red-tailed hawk, and turkey vulture.

Viewing Information: A maintenance path leads from lower parking lot to viewing area and blind. Best viewing is during daylight hours, year-round. Or, from parking lot scan woodland clearing for deer. Barrier-free fishing pier and swimming beach.

Directions: From Cumberland Parkway near Glasgow, travel south 2.5 miles on US 31E. Turn right on KY 252 and drive 11 miles to Quarry Road entrance on left.

Ownership: U.S. Army Corps of Engineers (502) 646-2055
Size: 1.5 acres   **Closest Town:** Glasgow

Description: Situated on 10,000-acre Barren River reservoir, this park contains 2,100 acres of hardwood forest, home to white-tailed deer, eastern cottontail rabbit, gray squirrel, red fox, raccoon, striped skunk, groundhog, and opossum. Hawks, several owl species, bobwhite, and a small population of wild turkey also live here.

Viewing Information: The state boat dock 2 miles from the park entrance is the primary viewing area. Winter is best for watching Canada geese and other waterfowl, and bald eagle along shoreline; several gull species also visit each year. Viewing is excellent on 1.5 miles of nature trails winding through hardwoods and a 2.5-mile paved bike/fitness trail that runs through woods, near the golf course, and along open fields. Common water snake and black racer are on the move in spring and summer, as are eastern bluebird and other migratory songbirds. Guided tours; recreation supervisor; full-service marina; 18-hole golf; horseback riding; beach; and pool (seasonal).

Directions: *From Cumberland Parkway at Glasgow, drive 11.5 miles south on US 31E to park entrance.*

Ownership: Kentucky Department of Parks (502) 646-2151
Size: 2,187 acres   **Closest Town:** Glasgow

S O U T H - C E N T R A L

Raccoons aren't afraid to get their feet wet. These ring-tailed bandits spend a great deal of time at the edges of ponds and streams foraging for fish, frogs, crayfish, as well as the eggs and young of birds. Raccoons prefer mature forests with some hollow trees.
JEFFREY A. BROWN

21. DRY CREEK UNIT, BARREN RIVER LAKE WMA

Description: Adjoining 10,000-acre Barren River Lake, this unit's bottomland fields host white-tailed deer, bobwhite quail, wild turkey, gray and fox squirrel, rabbit, and various bird species year-round.

Viewing Information: Best viewing is from a barrier-free platform near entrance where food is used to attract wildlife. Early mornings in spring are best for viewing (or hearing) turkeys. A half-mile gravel trail leads to lake where various waterbirds and, on occasion, migrating waterfowl may be seen. *HUNTING ALLOWED IN DESIGNATED AREAS.* Lodging, restaurant, and seasonal camping at nearby Barren River State Resort Park.

Directions: *From Cumberland Parkway at Glasgow, drive 11.5 miles south on US 31E to KY 87 across from entrance to Barren River State Resort Park. Turn east (left) on KY 87 and travel 4.9 miles through town of Austin. Turn south on Bradshaw Road, drive 3.6 miles, and turn right onto 1-lane gravel road. Parking and cedar-sided viewing shed are near bottom of hill.*

Ownership: U.S. Army Corps of Engineers; leased to Kentucky Department of Fish and Wildlife Resources (502) 842-0056
Size: 900 acres   **Closest Town:** Glasgow

22. DALE HOLLOW LAKE STATE PARK

Description: On 27,700-acre Dale Hollow Lake, this site is known for its wintering bald eagle, many white-tailed deer and wild turkey, and raccoon, gray fox, and squirrel. Rolling terrain features hardwoods, boulder slopes, and waterfalls, and supports a wide variety of plants.

Viewing Information: Viewing is good along the 3-mile park road, a 1-mile road to the picnic shelter, and more than 20 miles of hiking/horseback trails. Year-round, look for bobwhite, wood duck, killdeer, red-tailed and broadwinged hawk, and barn and screech owl. Muskrat and weasel are common year-round. Wildflower viewers can enjoy maypop, wild rhododendron, wild rose, dogwood, honeysuckle, and curly dock. Eagles Point and other overlooks offer panoramic lake views. Visitor center; full-service marina. Special events and daily programs Memorial Day to Labor Day.

Directions: *From Burkesville, take KY 90 east to KY 449. Drive south 4.6 miles to KY 1206, then 3.7 miles to park entrance.*

Ownership: Kentucky Department of Parks
(502) 433-7431
Size: 3, 398 Acres   **Closest Town:** Burkesville

Eastern bluebirds raise 2-3 broods each year in nest sites chosen by the male. Each clutch contains 4-6 pale blue eggs. Incubation takes about two weeks and the youngsters fly in another 15-18 days. Favorite foods of this songbird include caterpillars, spiders, and soft fruits. JEFFREY A. BROWN

Rose-breasted Grosbeak

Red-eyed Vireo

Yellow-breasted Chat

THE BLUEGRASS STATE'S TROPICAL TRAVELERS

Many songbirds that nest in Kentucky's summer woodlands and fields are tropical travelers. More than half of the bird species that breed in Kentucky migrate as far south as Mexico, the Caribbean Islands and Central and South America to spend the winter. Birds such as warblers, swallows, flycatchers, hummingbirds, buntings, orioles, bobolinks, common nighthawks and the species pictured here travel these great distances twice a year.

Populations of neotropical migrants are declining. Causes are unclear. One factor may be habitat loss in the form of broken patches of forests in wintering areas, breeding grounds and along travel routes.

Summer Tanager

Wood Thrush

Wearing more drab colors in their winter homes, the yellow-breasted chat chooses Central America for winter living while the red-eyed vireo finds South America to its liking. Summer tanagers spend the winter in both Central and South America. Although the rose-breasted grosbeak travels the farthest south of any species pictured, it shares the northern portion of its wintering range (represented by hash marks on map) with the wood thrush.

PackHill '94

Kentucky is cooperating with Tennessee and Alabama in monitoring neotropical migrants. Kentucky birders proficient in identifying bird sounds may volunteer to work in the monitoring program by writing KDFWR, #1 Game Farm Rd., Frankfort, KY 40601. Landowners involved in forest stewardship or the KDFWR's habitat improvement program are also invited to participate.

23. LAKE CUMBERLAND STATE RESORT PARK

Description: Located on 50,250-acre Lake Cumberland, this site is known for numerous white-tailed deer, raccoon, gray fox, striped skunk, and gray squirrel. Upland hardwood forest provides spring and summer homes for migratory songbirds such as scarlet tanager, eastern bluebird, titmouse, vireos, wrens, chickadees, goldfinches, and a variety of warblers. Wildflowers such as phlox, fire pink, and lily dot the park.

Viewing Information: Primary viewing is along 5-mile entrance drive to lodge. Viewing deck behind lodge offers a vista of the lake and close-up chances to see raccoon and gray fox. Mallard and bald eagle may be observed along lake shoreline in winter; summer visitors include several gull species. Nature center offers a full-time naturalist, guided tours, additional viewing information, and access to a 4-mile loop nature trail. Special events throughout year, daily programs Memorial Day to Labor Day. Full-service marina; horseback riding (seasonal).

Directions: From Jamestown, drive 8 miles south on US 127 to park entrance.

Ownership: Kentucky Department of Parks (502) 343-3111
Size: 3,117 acres   **Closest Town:** Jamestown

24. WOLF CREEK NATIONAL FISH HATCHERY

Description: Surrounded by upland pine forest with cool-water streams, this site provides opportunities to see rainbow and brown trout in the hatchery and white-tailed deer on the grounds. Great blue heron and belted kingfisher fish for dinner here.

Viewing Information: Deer venture onto face of dam to feed every evening, year-round. Best viewing is from northeast corner of front parking lot; bring a lawn chair. Hatchery contains interpretive displays, drinking fountains, and barrier-free restrooms; open 7 a.m. to 3:30 p.m. daily. Closed Christmas Day. Barrier-free fishing area on hatchery outfall ditch. Camping nearby.

Directions: The hatchery is 12 miles south of Jamestown on US 127. Follow signs to hatchery.

Ownership: U.S. Fish & Wildlife Service (502) 343-3797
Size: 19 acres   **Closest Town:** Jamestown

25. CUMBERLAND FALLS STATE RESORT PARK

Description: Secluded within 300,000 acres of Daniel Boone National Forest, the abundant wildlife of this park include white-tailed deer, bobcat, gray fox, raccoon, gray squirrel, and wild turkey. The mixture of pines and hardwoods along steep slopes also attracts such birds as woodpeckers (8 species, including the federally-listed endangered red-cockaded), red-shouldered hawk, and migratory songbirds, including many warblers—the black and white, and Kentucky. The park is also bordered by 4.5 miles of a Kentucky Wild River section of the Cumberland River, used by mallard, wood duck, and beaver.

Viewing Information: Sixteen miles of widespread trails lead through distinct forest communities. Canoe floats through the park during summer and fall can be an enjoyable way to see wildlife. A large patio directly behind lodge offers a 2-mile vista of Cumberland River gorge where red-tailed and broad-winged hawk soar almost daily. Plant lovers can enjoy several species of trillium (erect, large-flowered, sessile, yellow, painted) and native orchid as well as mountain laurel, dogwood, redbud, and rosebay rhododendron. Brochures/visitor guides available at lodge; year-round naturalist program and museum; daily interpretive programs (Memorial Day to Labor Day); special events (September-May); swimming pool; horseback riding (seasonal); canoe rental.

Directions: *From I-75 at Corbin/Cumberland Falls exit, drive 8 miles west on US 25W to KY 90. Follow KY 90 for 7 miles to park entrance.*

Ownership: Kentucky Department of Parks (606) 528-4121
Size: 1,794 acres   **Closest Town:** Corbin

Early spring bloomers, dogwood and redbud are especially beautiful emerging from woodlands not yet fully dressed in green. Dogwood berries provide fall and winter food for deer and many songbird species. GENE BOAZ

Description: This remote, rugged, and wild area where black bear are returning and river otter have been reintroduced boasts a diversity of plants and wildlife. Sandstone cliffs are home to unique, specially adapted flora and fauna. Waters of the Big South Fork host nearly 70 species of fish, including walleye. The South Fork of the Cumberland River from the KY-TN line to Blue Heron is a Kentucky Wild River. The historic mining community of Blue Heron has been redeveloped to tell the story of life in a company mining town. In addition to the services noted in the icons below, Blue Heron offers food services from April-October, interpretive displays, mammal/bird checklists, and river access. Alum Ford offers primitive camping, boat docks, and hiking trails. Yahoo Falls features scenic waterfall and overlook.

Viewing Information: Wildlife may be viewed year-round with moderate chances of seeing white-tailed deer. From Bear Creek, Devils Jump, and gorge overlooks, watch for migrating raptors, including broad-winged and red-shouldered hawk, in September and October. *OPEN TO HUNTING; EXERCISE CAUTION DURING BIG GAME SEASON.* Consult Blue Heron staff for hunting dates and also whitewater safety precautions. *SOME 4X4 ROADS MAY BE IMPASSABLE IN BAD WEATHER.*

Directions: *See map at right. From junction of US 27 and KY 1651 near Whitley City, proceed west through Stearns and east on KY 92 to Revelo. Turn right on KY 742 for 9.5 miles to Blue Heron.*

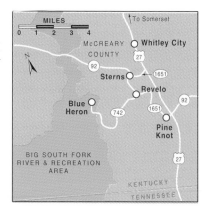

Ownership: National Park Service (606) 376-3787 (Blue Heron)
Size: 34,000 acres in Kentucky
Closest Town: Revelo

Jesse Stuart called Kentucky America's heart. Distant from coastal waters, this heartland has recorded 14 seagull species: the Bonaparte's, California, common black-headed, Franklin's, glaucous, great black-backed, lesser black-backed, herring, Iceland, laughing, little, ring-billed, Sabine's, and Thayer's. Although frequenting Cave Run Lake and the Ohio River, gulls concentrate at Kentucky and Barkley lakes.

27. WESLY BEND UNIT, LAKE CUMBERLAND MARSH PROJECT

Description: This waterfowl refuge on Cumberland Lake WMA features bottomland hardwoods, freshwater marsh, warm-water streams, and cropland.

Viewing Information: In summer and early fall, hikers may see wild turkey, white-tailed deer. Look for woodpeckers and red-tailed and Cooper's hawk in summer. *AREA CLOSES OCTOBER 15 THROUGH MARCH 15;* look for mallard, black and wood duck, and teal outside closure. No barrier-free acess. *USE CAUTION DURING HUNTING SEASONS.*

Directions: *From Somerset, drive 4.3 miles west on KY 1674, turn left onto Clifty Rd. Drive 1.6 miles, turn left onto Beech Grove Rd. for 0.4 mile, then turn right onto Wesly Rd. and travel 1.1 miles to parking area.*

Ownership: U.S. Army Corps of Engineers; managed by Kentucky Department of Fish and Wildlife Resources (606) 376-8083
Size: 68 acres **Closest Town:** Somerset

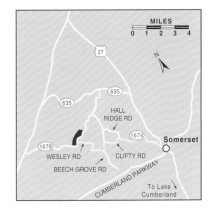

28. GREEN RIVER LAKE WMA

Description: Surrounding Green River Lake, more than half of this WMA is forested. The site is home to white-tailed deer, wild turkey, eastern cottontail rabbit, bobwhite, and squirrel. Watch for eastern bluebird, and yellow-shafted flicker in uplands; mallard, pintail, Canada goose, great blue heron, and bald eagle favor ponds and lakes. Field daisy, black-eyed susan, blue phlox, water lily, blackberry, and goldenrod bloom spring and summer.

Viewing Information: Best viewing is from Wildlife Observation Center at the upper Green River Unit. From barrier-free blind on the wetland, view shorebirds and waterfowl in winter and red-winged blackbird, other songbirds in spring and summer.

Directions: *From Campbellsville drive 4 miles east on KY 70, then south 14.2 miles on KY 76, and turn right at "Wildlife Observation Center" sign onto gravel road. Blind is 0.2 mile on right.*

Ownership: U.S. Army Corps of Engineers; managed by Kentucky Department of Fish and Wildlife Resources (502) 465-5039
Size: 20,500 acres **Closest Town:** Campbellsville

REGION THREE: NORTH-CENTRAL

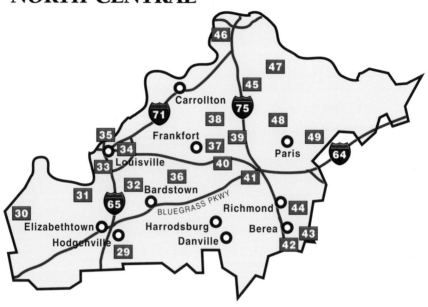

Site 29 Abraham Lincoln Birthplace National Historic Site
Site 30 Yellowbank WMA
Site 31 Otter Creek Park
Site 32 Bernheim Arboretum and Research Forest
Site 33 Jefferson County Memorial Forest
Site 34 Beargrass Creek State Nature Preserve
Site 35 Caperton Swamp
Site 36 Taylorsville Lake State Park and WMA
Site 37 Kentucky Fish and Wildlife Game Farm
Site 38 Kleber WMA
Site 39 Frankfort Fish Hatchery
Site 40 Buckley Wildlife Sanctuary
Site 41 Raven Run Nature Sanctuary
Site 42 Owsley Fork Reservoir, Berea College Forest
Site 43 Indian Fort Mountain Trails Area, Berea College Forest
Site 44 Central Kentucky WMA
Site 45 Lloyd WMA
Site 46 Big Bone Lick State Park
Site 47 Kincaid Lake State Park
Site 48 Quiet Trails State Nature Preserve
Site 49 Clay WMA

Description: Oak-hickory forests, an old-growth grove, and meadows host white-tailed deer, wild turkey, bobwhite, migratory songbirds, squirrel, raccoon, opossum, and groundhog.

Viewing Information: Best viewing is along 2.2 miles of trails during spring, fall, and winter when vegetation is less lush. Look for deer year-round; spring is best for cardinal, eastern bluebird, blue jay, and woodpecker. Red-tailed hawk is seen spring and winter. Visitor center; boardwalk; sinking spring; guided tours by reservation.

Directions: *From Elizabethtown, drive 10 miles south on KY 61 (Lincoln Parkway) to Hodgenville. Continue south 2 miles on US 31E/KY 61 to park entrance.*

Ownership: National Park Service (502) 358-3137
Size: 116.5 acres   **Closest Town:** Hodgenville

Description: On the Ohio River, this WMA holds oak-hickory and beech-maple forests sprinkled with persimmon, dogwood, redbud, sassafras, autumn olive, American plum, and pines. Look for white-tailed deer, wild turkey, wood duck, rabbit, bobwhite, raccoon, red and gray fox, and beaver. Nesting and migrant birds include American kestrel, four swallow species, white-breasted nuthatch, northern shoveler, wood duck, and killdeer.

Viewing Information: Best viewing is in spring and summer along 8 miles of roads with turn-outs. Additional viewing on 5 miles of KY 259. More than 20 miles of mowed-grass paths offer excellent birding. Abundant wildflowers in spring/late summer include unique occurrences of the purple fingless orchid, Lady Tresses orchid, large-flowered trillium, and swamp yellow. *VEHICLES NOT ALLOWED OFF ROAD. OPEN TO HUNTING; CHECK SEASON DATES.*

Directions: *From Brandenburg at the intersection of KY 1051 and US 79, drive 2.4 miles south on US 79 and turn west on KY 144. Drive 17.8 miles to KY 259, then 7 miles to WMA check station on right just after crossing Yellowbank Creek and passing camping area.*

Ownership: Kentucky Department of Fish and Wildlife Resources (502) 547-6856
Size: 6,000 acres   **Closest Town:** Hardinsburg

NORTH-CENTRAL

31. OTTER CREEK PARK

Description: This educational nature park adjacent to Fort Knox contains an excellent variety of native mammals and birds and more than 4,000 varieties of native and exotic plants. (Wild ginger, sessile trillium, twin-leaf wood poppy, jewelweed, ferns, and persimmon tree are only a few.) Primarily forested in hardwoods, the park contains a freshwater marsh, cool- and warm-water streams, cropland, and pasture.

Viewing Information: Viewing opportunities are available year-round, daylight to dark. Residents to watch for include white-tailed deer, groundhog, raccoon, striped skunk, opossum, chipmunk, bat, and squirrel. Paved roads offer good viewing from cars. Three hiking trails and open pipeline areas provide access to wildlife and plants in various ecosystems. Fees for some activities; 2 picnic areas charge small entry fee per vehicle. Park contains 3 old villages, mills, cemeteries, and Morgan's cave. Staffed interpretive center; guided/self-guided tours; horse trails.

Directions: From Louisville take I-65 south to I-265 west. Turn left (south) onto US 31W to Muldraugh. Turn right (west) at stoplight on KY 1638, travel 2.8 miles to park entrance. Visitor center is 0.9 mile from entrance.

Ownership: City of Louisville (502) 583-3577 or (502) 942-3641
Size: 3,000 acres   **Closest Town:** Muldraugh

An opportunistic pursuer of voles, mice, fruit, grasses, and corn, the red fox inhabits open meadows and farmlands, often denning near people. Although a litter may contain 2-10 pups, the average is five. Its slightly smaller cousin, the cat-like gray fox, prefers a woodlands habitat. GENE BOAZ

Description: This site consists primarily of upland oak-hickory forest with maple, beech, birch, and mixed pines, and contains warm-water streams, reservoirs, ponds, cropland, and wildlife food plots. White-tailed deer, bobwhite, wild turkey, hognose snake, rabbit, and squirrel are just a few of the area's year-round residents. View numerous migratory birds, from waterfowl to summer-dwelling songbirds, including the bufflehead, black duck, American wigeon, Philadelphia vireo, and Bewick's wren. Bernheim Arboretum Center offers 2,500 developed acres with more than 1,800 varieties of native and exotic plants. Visit the nature center to see white-tailed deer and birds of prey, and exhibits of small animals, reptiles, fish, and aquatic life.

Viewing Information: Developed area is open March 15 to November 15. Many species are visible from roads open to cars or from gravel fire roads where only walking is permitted. Trails throughout area offer viewing in various ecosystems. Trail system expansion, signage, and corresponding interpretive brochures are recent improvements. Public lake offers fishing. Weekend/holiday entry fee charged per vehicle. KOA campground at Shepherdsville.

Directions: *From Shepherdsville, take I-65 south to Clermont and exit 112 (KY 245). Turn left (east) on KY 245 and travel 1 mile to main entrance on right.*

Ownership: Isaac W. Bernheim Foundation
(502) 543-2451 or (502) 955-8512
Size: 14,000 acres   **Closest Town:** Clermont

NORTH-CENTRAL

Common except in dense eastern forests, bobwhites live in groups called coveys. Resting in brushy cover, birds circle with heads facing outward to protect against predators and capitalize on body heat. Hens nest singly in concealed hollows lined with grass. Best bobwhite viewing: Central/West Kentucky WMAs.
GENE BOAZ

45

Description: Divided into four distinct tracts, this forest contains upland oak-hickory and bottomland hardwoods. The area is home to bobwhite, wild turkey, white-tailed deer, bobcat, coyote, woodcock, beaver, muskrat, and mink. The forest fills with migratory songbirds during spring and summer, and trillium, fern, lily, orchid, and iris grow on the forest floor.

Viewing Information: Best viewing is spring through fall, especially for mallard, wood duck, Canada goose, great blue and green heron, American kestrel, and red-shouldered and red-tailed hawk. Blinds, platforms, towers, and foot trails are available. Most roads are paved. Veterans Memorial Trail is barrier-free and has interpretive displays. Forest Welcome Center, 11311 Mitchell Hill Rd., open daily 8 a.m. to 5:30 p.m. Guided/self-guided tours; horse trails; fishing pier. Small entrance fee to Horine Section. Canoe access.

Directions: See map below. From Louisville, take I-65 south to I-265/KY 841 (Gene Snyder Expressway) west. Take New Cut Road exit 6. Turn left on Manslick Road and travel 1.4 miles to Mitchell Hill Road (flashing lights). Turn right and travel 1 mile to intersection of Mitchell Hill and Holsclaw roads. Turn left and follow Holsclaw Road 1.5 miles to top of hill. Make sharp right turn onto park road and follow to ranger station.

Ownership: Jefferson County; managed by Louisville/Jefferson County Parks Department (502) 368-5404
Size: 5,123 acres   **Closest Town:** Fairdale

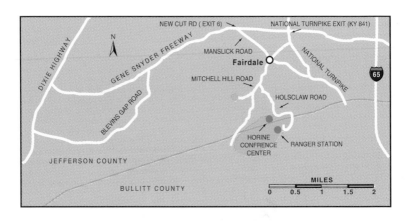

Description: This natural area nestled in the center of Louisville offers urban dwellers opportunities to hike and leave the city behind. The preserve contains more than 180 species of trees, shrubs, and flowering plants. Although the woods appear very "weedy" due to Japanese honeysuckle, plant diversity is rich for so small an area. Wooded uplands (black cherry, locust, walnut, beech) and floodplain woods (sycamore, ash, maple) host more than 150 species of birds. The site is well-known by local birders for a diversity of warblers during spring and fall migrations, including the orange-crowned, cerulean, and yellow-breasted chat. Other songbirds include the olive-sided flycatcher and eastern wood peewee. The area is home to great horned and screech owls, and Kirkland's water snake, a sensitive species.

Viewing Information: Watch for wildlife from 1 mile of trails and a boardwalk. Viewing migrating songbirds and great blue and green heron is best in early spring and fall. Look for great egret in summer and black-crowned and yellow-crowned night heron, Canada goose, black and wood duck, flycatchers, and 6 woodpecker species in spring and summer. Killdeer, lesser golden plover, lesser yellowlegs, spotted sandpiper, common snipe, and woodcock also visit in spring. Activity/tour schedule, bird checklist available on request from Louisville Nature Center.

Directions: *In Louisville, from junction of I-264 (Watterson Expressway) and Newburg Road (KY 1703), follow Newburg Road north for 1 mile. Turn left onto Trevilian Way for 0.5 mile. Turn right into Joe Creason Park.*

Ownership: Kentucky State Nature Preserves Commission; managed by Louisville Nature Center (502) 458-1328

Size: 41 acres   **Closest Town:** Louisville

NORTH-CENTRAL

Kentucky's only flying mammals are man's best friend. Bats eat vast quantities of insects, especially mosquitoes. Red, big brown, and little brown bats are the most common of 14 bat species in the state. Kentucky bats on the federal list of endangered species include the Virginia big-eared, Indiana, gray, southeastern, and eastern small-footed.

Description: Less than 5 miles from the heart of downtown Louisville, this small preserve offers peaceful respite for urban dwellers. A grassy path leads to a hidden pond and wetland area that hosts wood duck, mallard, blue-winged teal, killdeer, common yellowthroat, and orchard oriole. More than 20 warbler species visit during spring and fall migrations. For several years, a pair of red-shouldered hawks has been seen nesting here, as have several pairs of prothonotary warblers. Rabbits routinely skirt the property edge; raccoon and white-tailed deer tracks are plentiful.

Viewing Information: Viewing probability, spring through fall, is moderate to high for waterfowl whenever there is standing water in the pond. Several species of sparrows use the grassy area leading to the pond; migratory songbirds are plentiful in trees along the pathway. Gravel parking area is 400 yards from pond. Cross the road to Cox's Park (0.1 mile west) to watch for grebes, common loon, and gulls on the Ohio River. *CAUTION: WHEN VIEWING RIVER, BE MINDFUL OF TRAFFIC; VIEW FROM SAFE PLACE.* Parking and restrooms available at Cox's Park.

Directions: *From I-71 in Louisville, take Zorn Avenue north about 0.2 mile, then River Road east for 1.3 miles to site.*

Ownership: Jefferson County; managed by Louisville/Jefferson County Parks Department (502) 456-8100
Size: 23 acres   **Closest Town:** Louisville

Restoration efforts are returning river otters to the eastern two-thirds of the state. Public releases, magnified by media attention, educate people about the behavior and habitat needs of these chocolate-colored, be-whiskered dwellers of slow-moving streams.
DENVER BRYAN

36. TAYLORSVILLE LAKE STATE PARK AND WMA

Description: It's not uncommon to see white-tailed deer, wild turkey, gray and red fox, groundhog, river otter, and squirrels at this site on 3,050-acre Taylorsville Lake. The park mainly consists of abandoned farmland dotted with woods. Songbirds such as the indigo bunting and western bluebird are plentiful. Red-shouldered hawk, barred owl, and osprey are also common here; many migratory waterfowl stop over, fall and winter.

Viewing Information: Best viewing is from park roads and popular 3-mile trail. WMA viewing area includes 20 acres of native prairie restoration and examples of backyard habitat. A short woodland walk and viewing station are available for wildlife watching and photography. Full-service marina.

Directions: From the junction of KY 44 and KY 55 east of Taylorsville, drive 5 miles east on KY 44 to KY 248. Continue on KY 248 for 2 miles to park entrance.

Ownership: U.S. Army Corps of Engineers; Kentucky Department of Parks; managed by Kentucky Department of Fish and Wildlife Resources (502) 477-9024 or (502) 477-8713

Size: 11,672 acres   **Closest Town:** Taylorsville

After the April-June breeding season, osprey parents take turns incubating 2-4 eggs for a little over a month. Lake Barkley offers excellent viewing of ospreys; the birds also frequent Taylorsville, Cave Run, and other large lakes during the warm months.
JEFFREY A. BROWN

NORTH-CENTRAL

49

CENTRAL KENTUCKY

RED-TAILED HAWK

RED CEDAR

REDBUD

MEADOWLARK

RED FOX

STRIPED SHINER

BLUE PHLOX

BULLFROG

FINGERNAIL CLAM

Central Kentucky's farmlands, fields and forests reflect their link to the original prairie and savanna (grassland with scattered large trees) vegetation of the area. Following roadways coursing along buffalo traces reveal remnant ash-oak savannas, cedar glades and prairie lands. Wildlife typical of the region, such as quail and cottontail rabbits, generally reflect evolving in an openland environment.

BUR OAK

EASTERN
BLUEBIRD

FOX SQUIRREL

BLACKHAW

PRAIRIE
CONEFLOWER

EASTERN
BOX TURTLE

LONGEAR
SUNFISH

SMALLMOUTH BASS

Pack Hill '94

The region is underlain mostly with limestone bedrock which caused the formation of many underground streams and cave systems. These host a variety of wildlife species specially adapted to live in a cavernous environment. Many of Kentucky's rarer forms of wildlife use special habitats found only in these cave systems.

Description: Established in 1945 to propagate game animals for release, this site is home base for the Kentucky Department of Fish and Wildlife Resources. No longer a game farm, this area is becoming a prime educational/recreational complex with the opening of Salato Wildlife Education Center slated for fall 1995. Mild to moderately sloping ridgetops combined with grasslands, mixed pine hardwoods, and oak-hickory woodlands are characteristic of the central Bluegrass. Watch for white-tailed deer, black bear, cougar, and captive herd of American bison. Warm weather brings scampering chipmunks. Near blinds, native grasses and wildflowers attract insects, which in turn draw the great-crested flycatcher in spring. Fall brings chipping sparrow, American goldfinch, and Carolina chickadee. Northern oriole, yellow-rumped warbler, and cedar waxwing visit spring/fall.

Viewing Information: Open year-round, sunrise to sunset. Deer often range along the eastern boundary. Resident flocks of Canada geese and mallards roam freely and nest here. Various waterfowl species and waterbirds visit during early spring and late fall migrations, including northern shoveler and black duck. Excellent birding on self-guided tours, spring through fall. Guided tours by appointment; scheduled educational programs. Some areas not open to public due to ongoing construction. *CAUTION: WALKERS FREQUENTLY USE PAVED 2-LANE ROADWAYS.* Two public fishing lakes; picnic shelters.

***Directions:** From I-64 at Frankfort, take exit 53 to US 127 north and travel 1.5 miles to left turn on US 60. Drive 1.7 miles west on US 60 to main entrance on right. Proceed to designated visitor parking. LIMITED BARRIER-FREE PARKING.*

Ownership: Kentucky Department of Fish and Wildlife Resources (502) 564-4336

Size: 132 acres   **Closest Town:** Frankfort

The KDFWR is increasingly involving constituency groups in planning programs which are funded solely by hunting and fishing licenses. Volunteers play a great part in the success of these programs. A variety of educational programs and activities along with print news and television programming are building a well-informed public from kids to seniors.

38. KLEBER WMA

Description: This site's main viewing area overlooks a 1-acre pond that supports white-tailed deer, wild turkey, doves, red-tailed hawk, American kestrel, great horned owl, ducks, and numerous small mammals such as red bat, eastern cottontail rabbit, chipmunk, and raccoon. Picturesque view from cedar-lined ridge features red and white oak on hillsides and along roadways.

Viewing Information: Early morning and late afternoon are best for viewing. The area hosts wood duck and mallard in fall and winter; spring and summer are best for seeing great blue heron and cattle egret. Area songbirds include robin, American goldfinch, and warbler species. *OPEN TO HUNTING; CHECK SEASON DATES.*

Directions: *See map at right. From Frankfort, travel north on US 127 (toward Owenton) for 8.5 miles to KY 2919 (Indian Gap Road). Turn right onto Indian Gap Road and travel 3 miles, past the Frankfort Fish Hatchery, to KY 1707. Turn left (north) and travel 2.4 miles to Mt. Vernon Road on left. Turn left and follow signs to viewing site. MT. VERNON ROAD IS 1-LANE, PAVED.*

Ownership: Kentucky Department of Fish and Wildlife Resources (502) 535-6335 or (502) 564-4858
Size: 2,228 acres
Closest Town: Stamping Ground

Most people associate bats with caves, but eastern red bats don't use caves—they roost in trees, giving the appearance of hanging leaves. Red bats hibernate in hollow trees.
JEFFREY A. BROWN

39. FRANKFORT FISH HATCHERY

Description: The Frankfort Fish Hatchery was built in the 1950s on land donated by the Kentucky Department of Fish and Wildlife Resources, and operated as a federal fish hatchery until 1986. The hatchery is situated on Elkhorn Creek where sycamore, box elder, walnut, and silver maple are abundant. Travelers approaching the site when it is hidden by lush vegetation may find it difficult to believe that the facility is nearby. The hatchery uses state-of-the-art equipment to produce channel catfish, bluegill, largemouth bass, hybrid striped bass, walleye, goldfish, and fathead minnows. Although no attempt is made to produce albino catfish, visitors can see specimens in several of the hatchery's 45 rearing ponds. A research project on freshwater mussels may also be viewed.

Viewing Information: Open Monday through Friday, 7 a.m. to 3 p.m., year-round. April, May, and June are best for observing hatchery in full operation. An outside display pool, maintained March to November, contains bass, bluegill, hybrid striped bass, trout, paddlefish, gar, carp, buffalo, crayfish, goldfish, several catfish species, frogs, and a snapping turtle. Wood duck, Canada goose, and wading birds such as great blue and little green heron are common here spring, summer, and fall. Osprey occasionally visit. The site is excellent for viewing American kestrel, orioles, swallows, and soaring vultures. Anglers can walk to Elkhorn Creek to fish from the banks (fishing license required). An 11-acre island, owned by the hatchery, splits the waterway. Self-guided tours; group tours by appointment. Barrier-free access to display pool and hatchery building.

Directions: *From Frankfort, travel north on US 127 (toward Owenton) 8.5 miles to KY 2919 (Indian Gap Road). Turn right for 1.5 miles to hatchery entrance on right. Follow paved road to display area. (See map, page 53)*

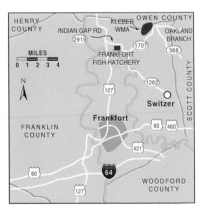

Ownership: Kentucky Department of Fish and Wildlife Resources (502) 564-4957 or (502) 564-3596
Size: 114 acres
Closest Town: Frankfort

40. BUCKLEY WILDLIFE SANCTUARY

Description: Nestled in the rolling hills of Woodford County, this site lies near the Kentucky River and holds oak, hickory, cedar, and cropland. From field thistle, buttercup, and figwort to lily, orchid, and ferns, the area is a virtual plant-viewing paradise. White-tailed deer, eastern cottontail rabbit, gray and fox squirrel, raccoon, groundhog, little brown bat, snapping and box turtle, fence lizard, northern spring peeper, and gray tree frog are common.

Viewing Information: Deer, fox squirrel, rose-breasted grosbeak, and hooded warbler are often seen along Germany Road to area. Excellent viewing is available in fields, forests, edges, and near pond on site. A blind offers good chances to view wildlife. Monthly environmental programs and events. Species checklists; 3 walking trails; nature center.

Directions: See map at right. From I-64 near Frankfort, take exit 58 and drive 0.3 mile east on US 60 to KY 1681. Turn right and travel 2.5 miles to KY 1659. Turn left and go 1.7 miles to KY 1964, then turn right for 1.1 miles to Germany Road. Turn right and drive 1.3 miles to sanctuary entrance on left.

Ownership: Woodford Bank & Trust Company, managed by National Audubon Society (606) 873-5711
Size: 275 acres
Closest Town: Frankfort

You may not notice the well-camouflaged gray tree frog unless you hear its loud trill. This dweller of mixed forests and temporary wetlands is most active May through October. During the mating season, males sing in full view at night from trunks and fallen branches before migrating to ponds for breeding.
GENE BOAZ

41. RAVEN RUN NATURE SANCTUARY

Description: Located on the Kentucky River Palisades, Raven Run is known for its scenic overlook of one of the state's three undeveloped limestone gorges and its spectacular display of spring wildflowers, such as blue-eyed mary, and the very rare putty-root orchid. The area also holds excellent examples of successional changes from old fields to mature forest and plant communities characteristic of limestone soils. Two creeks, Raven Run and Chandler Creek, pass through the park.

Viewing Information: White-tailed deer may be seen most any time of day, year-round; best times are early mornings and late afternoons, especially on rainy days in winter. Primitive camping offered as part of guided program; small fee charged for guided tour. Free maps at nature center. Paved Freedom Trail offers barrier-free access. *CAUTION: HUNTING ALLOWED OUTSIDE PARK; DO NOT CROSS PARK BOUNDARIES DURING DEER SEASONS. TRAIL PORTIONS MAY BE CLOSED DURING WINTER.* Ferry at end of Tates Creek Road will transport cars across Kentucky River for a fee.

Directions: *From Circle 4 (commonly called New Circle Road, a beltline around Lexington), take exit 18 onto KY 1974 south (Tates Creek Road). Drive 9.5 miles to KY 1975 (Spears Road), turn left, and drive 1.6 miles to end of Spears Road. Turn right on KY 1976 (Jacks Creek Pike) and drive 1.5 miles to park on left. CAUTION: JACKS CREEK PIKE IS 2-LANE BUT NARROW. OCCASIONAL DENSE MORNING FOG; WATCH FOR SLOW-MOVING FARM MACHINERY, WILDLIFE CROSSING ROADS.*

Ownership: Lexington-Fayette Urban County Government (606) 272-6105 or (606) 288-2900

Size: 376 acres   **Closest Town:** Lexington

 Striped skunks seldom hurry, perhaps because they have few natural enemies except the great horned owl. Mortality is high, however. Roadways with carrion attract the nocturnal creatures, especially during the late winter breeding season. One litter per year usually contains five offspring born in May. In single file, young skunks travel behind the mother, who teaches them to hunt.

42. OWSLEY FORK RESERVOIR, BEREA COLLEGE FOREST

Description: An oak-hickory-pine and cove forest along this reservoir serves as a backdrop for spectacular courtship flights of woodcocks in winter. The area also holds raccoon, groundhog, opossum, striped skunk, and eastern cottontail rabbit. Watch for beaver and muskrat near shoreline.

Viewing Information: Viewing areas, open sunrise to sunset year-round, are gravel parking lot and portion of KY 21 along lakeshore of Owsley Fork Reservoir. (All other forest areas are closed to the public.) Open viewing areas offer chance to see gulls and loons in winter as well as wood duck, green heron, and Canada goose. Winter viewing is best for broad-winged hawk, barred owl, turkey vulture, and osprey. Watch for Kentucky warbler, pileated woodpecker, and wood thrush year-round. Self-guided tours on roads. Lake open to paddle craft, electric motors.

Directions: *From I-75, take exit 76 and travel 9 miles east on KY 21 to gravel parking area beside Owsley Fork Reservoir.*

Ownership: Berea College (606) 986-9341 ext. 5587
Size: 151 acres (reservoir)   **Closest Town:** Berea

43. INDIAN FORT MOUNTAIN TRAILS AREA, BEREA COLLEGE FOREST

Description: An interesting feature of this 7,800-acre upland hardwood forest demonstrates just how dynamic forests are. In 1987, an intense fire burned more than 800 wooded acres. Loss of the tree canopy allowed sunlight to penetrate to the forest floor, encouraging prairie and early successional vegetation where many neotropical migrant songbirds rest and feed. The forest supports numerous wildflowers, including pink lady slipper, showy orchid, and crested iris. In late winter woodcock mating flights are common in old fields.

Viewing Information: Migrant songbirds include summer tanager and chestnut-sided warbler. Open sunrise to sunset, year-round. Self-guided tours on 8 miles of trails. Trail map and bird checklist available upon request. Only the picnic area is barrier-free. *CAUTION: VIEWING FROM HEAVILY-TRAVELED KY 21 IS DANGEROUS, DIFFICULT, AND NOT ADVISED.*

Directions: *From I-75 south of Berea, take exit 76, turn east on KY 21, and travel 4.7 miles to entrance of Indian Fort parking lot.*

Ownership: Berea College (606) 986-9341 ext. 5587
Size: 500 acres (trails area)   **Closest Town:** Berea

44. CENTRAL KENTUCKY WMA

Description: Flat to gently rolling terrain holds old fields, croplands, cedar thickets, farm ponds, temporary streams, and small oak-hickory stands along ridge slopes. The Batch's burrowing crayfish, known to exist only in Madison, Estill, and Garrard counties, is found here. The area supports fox and gray squirrel, dove, eastern cottontail rabbit, opossum, bobwhite, and white-tailed deer. Also watch for wild turkey, coyote, red and gray fox, muskrat, mink, and a great variety of songbirds: Swainson's thrush, northern parula, and blue-winged warbler. Turkey vulture, sharp-shinned and Cooper's hawk, and great horned owl are fairly common. On occasion, grouse and woodcock are seen. Waterfowl frequent farm ponds where wood duck nest.

Viewing Information: No drive-through roads; walking is only way to see most of area on self-guided tours. Gravel parking areas (not barrier-free) are located throughout the area; wildlife may be viewed from vehicles in and around demonstration areas. Best viewing is during spring and fall, in morning and early evening. Dirt chimneys built by Batch's burrowing crayfish are scattered in the field surrounding the headquarters building. Restrooms available only during scheduled activities.

Directions: *From I-75 near Richmond, take exit 87 East (Richmond) onto KY 876, and drive 2.8 miles to US 421/25 South. Turn right (south) onto US 421/25 and travel 3.5 miles to split of US 421/25. Bear left onto US 421 and drive 3.2 miles to Dreyfus Rd. Turn left on Dreyfus Rd. for 2 miles to WMA entrance.*

Ownership: Kentucky Department of Fish and Wildlife Resources (606) 986-4130

Size: 1,690 acres   **Closest Town:** Richmond (north), Berea (south)

Gray squirrels helped settle Kentucky. They were (and are) abundant game, providing tasty meals. This member of the rodent family is an entertaining resident of most college campuses, city parks, and suburban streets. Nests on forked branches high in trees are spherical with a side entrance.
GENE BOAZ

Description: Farmland, brush, and one of the state's oldest virgin tree stands are home to dove, squirrel, rabbit, quail, groundhog, white-tailed deer, wild turkey, red and gray fox, red-tailed hawk, American kestrel, pileated woodpecker, and eastern bluebird.

Viewing Information: Viewing is best at rear of WMA on 4 miles of dirt roads and trails. Wildflowers, prairie grasses, and giant hardwoods attract songbirds and butterflies. Visitor center open during scheduled events; small fishing lake with barrier-free pier. *OPEN TO HUNTING; CHECK SEASON DATES.* Campgrounds nearby.

Directions: *From Crittenden, drive 1 mile south on US 25 and turn left on KY 491. Cross railroad tracks, take first left, and go 0.2 mile to clubhouse/parking area.*

Ownership: Kentucky Department of Fish and Wildlife Resources (606) 428-2262
Size: 1,179 acres   **Closest Town:** Crittenden

46. BIG BONE LICK STATE PARK

Description: This site, where great herds of giant mastodons, mammoths, and buffalo once drank from salt springs, is one of the most significant paleological sites in the United States.

Viewing Information: Look for white-tailed deer and captive bison along barrier-free, 0.4-mile Diorama Trail. Displays feature mammals that lived here 10,000 years ago. From a 2-mile loop trail winding around a 7-acre lake, look for wild turkey, red-winged blackbird, wood thrush, white-tailed deer, and gray and fox squirrel. Park brochure; guided tours in summer; self-guided tours; interpretive programs Labor Day-Memorial Day; fishing; picnic shelter; pool; grocery.

Directions: *From I-75 at Richwood, take exit 175 to KY 338, then west for 8 miles to park entrance.*

Ownership: Kentucky Department of Parks (606) 384-3522
Size: 525 acres   **Closest Town:** Union

NORTH-CENTRAL

Description: On 183-acre Kincaid Lake, these former farmlands and stands of maple, beech, birch, oak, and cedar harbor waterfowl, white-tailed deer, raccoon, red fox, gray squirrel, and chipmunk. Wrens, American goldfinch, eastern bluebird, and various warblers, including yellow-throated, use the area.

Viewing Information: Primary viewing is along entrance drive to the camp station. From the pool parking lot, watch for mallard, Canada goose, grebe, great blue heron, and crane on the lake year-round. Recreation center has information about other viewing locations in park; 2.5-mile nature trail begins here. Spring, summer, and fall provide best chances to view black snake and box turtle. Look for wild turkey in spring and fall. Self-guided tours; interpretive center; barrier-free fishing pier; pool; grocery.

Directions: *From I-75 at Williamstown, take exit 154. Follow KY 22 east to US 27, then south to Falmouth. From Falmouth take KY 159 north 4 miles to park entrance.*

Ownership: Kentucky Department of Parks (606) 654-3531
Size: 850 acres   **Closest Town:** Falmouth

Capable of reaching 200 mph in its predatory dives, the peregrine falcon snatches other birds in mid-air. Once Kentucky's high cliff nesters, peregrines are being released in cities where tall buildings and ledges resemble their natural habitat. Peregrines are wandering birds, sometimes seen at prime hawk-viewing sites in the Cumberland Mountains.
JOHN HENDRICKSON

Description: Ridges and ravines here border the main channel of the Licking River where more than 20 mussel species have been identified. Three miles of trails pass through old fields and maturing oak-hickory woods to the riverbank. The red-tailed hawk and saw-whet owl use the area, as do eastern cottontail rabbit, gray squirrel, raccoon, groundhog, vole, and white-footed mouse. More than 100 species (each) of birds, wildflowers, and trees have been recorded here.

Viewing Information: Trails throughout the preserve provide opportunities to observe migratory songbirds in spring and fall. Bluebird boxes are maintained along trails. Food plots attract wildlife, which may be viewed from a blind about 400 yards from parking lot. In late summer, open fields are awash with color of wildflowers. Look for Christmas fern in ravines. Along riverbanks, great blue and little blue heron, spotted sandpiper, and horned grebe may be viewed in fall. Fact sheet/species list; observation blind; self-guided tours.

Directions: *From Cynthiana, take US 27 north for 10.5 miles. Turn right onto KY 1284 and drive 2.7 miles to Sunrise, continue on Pugh's Ferry Road. After crossing 4-way intersection, drive 1.8 miles to preserve on right. CAUTION: PUGH'S FERRY ROAD IS VERY NARROW.*

Ownership: Kentucky State Nature Preserves
Commission (502) 573-2886
Size: 110 acres **Closest Town:** Cynthiana

NORTH-CENTRAL

The yellow-rumped warbler doesn't breed in the state, but regularly winters in various habitats near cedars and fruit-bearing trees. Kentucky claims 35 warbler species; most are neotropical migrants that nest in special habitats. The cerulean warbler, for example, chooses forest interiors, while the prothonotary warbler favors wetlands. GENE BOAZ

49. CLAY WMA

Description: With steep to rolling terrain, this area contains more than 3,000 woodland acres in maple, oak, hickory, beech, and cedar. Remaining portions consist of idle fields, wildlife food plots, croplands, and a small fishing lake. White-tailed deer, squirrel, eastern cottontail rabbit, raccoon, groundhog, opossum, striped skunk, bobwhite, wild turkey, and woodcock live here year-round. Coyote, bobcat, and red and gray fox also frequent the area, but are more difficult to spot.

Viewing Information: Viewing is from roadways on 2 units, each with 2.5 miles of gravel road. Gravel parking area can accommodate buses. Self-guided nature walk features food/wildflower plots, bluebird boxes, warm-season grasses, and autumn olive. Wood duck are common in spring; mallard in fall. Summer is best for red-tailed and broad-winged hawk and turkey vulture.

Directions: From the intersection of KY 36 and KY 32 in Carlisle, drive 6.4 miles east on KY 32 to KY 3315 (Cassidy Creek Road). Turn right (south) onto KY 3315 and travel 1.9 miles to lower unit. CAUTION: NARROW 1-LANE BRIDGE ON KY 3315. Upper unit is 1.9 miles further on KY 3315.

Ownership: Kentucky Department of Fish and Wildlife Resources (606) 289-2564
Size: 4,901 acres   **Closest Town:** Carlisle

Fish are one of Kentucky's most important natural resources.While fish reared in hatcheries are used to enhance some populations, they are no substitute for natural reproduction and quality habitat.

REGION FOUR: EASTERN

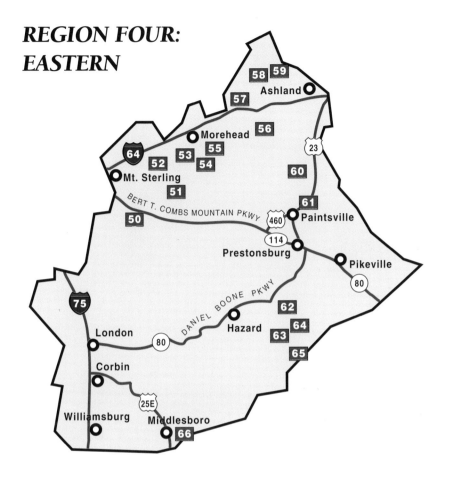

Site 50 Natural Bridge State Resort Park
Site 51 Gladie Creek Historic Site, Red River Gorge
Site 52 Zilpo Recreation Area
Site 53 Twin Knobs Campground
Site 54 Shallow Flats Observation Area
Site 55 Minor Clark Fish Hatchery
Site 56 Grayson Lake Nature Trail and WMA
Site 57 Carter Caves State Resort Park
Site 58 Greenbo Lake State Resort Park
Site 59 Jesse Stuart State Nature Preserve
Site 60 Yatesville Lake WMA Wetlands Viewing Area
Site 61 Paintsville Lake State Park and WMA
Site 62 Littcarr Wildlife Viewing Area
Site 63 Lilley Cornett Woods
Site 64 Kingdom Come State Park
Site 65 Little Shepherd Trail
Site 66 Hensley Settlement, Cumberland Gap National Historic Park

50. NATURAL BRIDGE STATE RESORT PARK

Description: The sandstone arch called Natural Bridge is only one of more than 150 natural stone arches within 5 miles of Hemlock Lodge. Natural Bridge isn't the largest, oldest, or even the most accessible arch in the area, but it is the most famous because it was developed as a tourist attraction in the 19th century. As the Appalachian Mountains were formed, this landscape rose hundreds of feet above sea level. Water runoff from higher elevations carved out the steep-walled canyon of Red River Gorge. Almost half of this park (994 acres) is managed as a state nature preserve in cooperation with the Kentucky State Nature Preserves Commission. The preserve protects forest communities representative of the Cumberland Plateau as well as habitat for the federally-listed endangered Virginia big-eared bat and the rare small-flowered yellow lady's slipper. The only developed facilities here are primitive hiking trails. *TO ENJOY AND PROTECT THE PRESERVE, TAKE EXTRA CARE TO STAY ON TRAIL.*

Viewing Information: Spring brings woodland warblers, including ovenbird and northern parula, and the sounds of wild turkey gobbling and ruffed grouse drumming. Pileated woodpecker live here year-round. Guided/self-guided tours; 18 miles of trails; interpretive center; slide programs; special annual events (such as Wildflower Weekend); activities brochure (weekly, April-October); canoe access; fishing; picnic shelters; swimming pool. *PARK IS CROWDED ON HOLIDAYS AND OCTOBER WEEKENDS.*

Directions: From Bert T. Combs Mountain Parkway east of Winchester, take exit 33 (Slade) and drive 2 miles south on KY 11 to park entrance.

Ownership: Kentucky Department of Parks (606) 663-2214
Size: 1,900 acres   **Closest Town:** Slade

With tail feathers spread into a fan, a male wild turkey struts his stuff, trying to entice one more female to join his harem. Thanks to restoration efforts, the state's wild turkey flock of a few hundred birds in the 1940s increased to more than 50,000 by the mid-1990s.
GENE BOAZ

Description: This historic site lies within the Red River Gorge Geologic Area, a National Natural Landmark recognized for its great diversity. Wildlife commonly seen in this upland cove forest of pines and mixed hardwoods are beaver, muskrat, little brown and small-footed bat, groundhog, skunk, squirrel, chipmunk, opossum, box turtle, vultures, red-tailed and broad-winged hawk, barred owl, crow, wood duck, and various songbirds, such as rufus-sided towhee and indigo bunting. Bobwhite, ruffed grouse, wild turkey, and woodcock are seen occasionally. Lucky visitors may glimpse a corn snake or great blue heron. The area also has a small captive bison herd. Red River, Kentucky's first National Wild and Scenic River, adjoins the site and Natural Bridge State Resort Park is nearby.

Viewing Information: *TO AVOID WEEKEND CROWDS,* best viewing is on weekdays in early morning and late afternoon during spring, summer, and fall. Visitor station, open 10 a.m. to 6 p.m., April through October, offers interpretive exhibits, brochures. Drinking water available; restrooms are not barrier-free. Viewing areas/blinds; restored log cabin; paved parking. Boat ramp on Red River. Camping nearby.

Directions: *From Bert T. Combs Mountain Parkway east of Winchester, take exit 33 (Slade) and drive north 0.1 mile on KY 11. Turn west on KY 15/11 for 1.5 miles, then north on KY 77 for 5.2 miles, then east on KY 715 for 3.5 miles to entrance.*

Ownership: USDA Forest Service (606) 663-2852
or (606) 745-3100
Size: 40 acres   **Closest Town:** Slade

The wood duck is a Kentucky cavity nester that adapts well to strategically-placed nest boxes in tree cover near large bodies of water. Whether or not nests are over water, wood duck hatchlings scamper out and plop 12-15 feet. GENE BOAZ

EASTERN

65

Description: Located on a peninsula jutting into Cave Run Lake, this site is primarily forested in oak-hickory and bottomland hardwoods. The area is home to white-tailed deer, wild turkey, groundhog, skunk, and opossum. The campground at the end of Zilpo Road, a National Scenic Byway, contains miles of hiking trails and paved loop roads.

Viewing Information: Best viewing of deer is May-September; does with fawns June-September. Deer are most visible in mowed fields during morning and evening. Great blue heron frequent the area in summer and various gulls, including Bonaparte's, are in evidence spring, fall, and winter; Canada goose common year-round. Bald eagle and osprey sometimes visit in winter. Various songbirds use the area, including red-eyed and white-eyed vireo, and yellow warbler. Chances to see or hear wild turkey are best when campground is quiet during early morning hours. Spring is best for viewing reptiles and amphibians in woodland ponds in campground. Paved roads and trails; RV parking; electric hook-ups; showers; boat landing; swimming beach with bath house; interpretive programs. Small entry fee charged per vehicle, half price with Golden Age Pass. Visitor center offers information on local wildlife viewing areas, species checklists. *CAMPGROUND CLOSED ONE FALL WEEKEND FOR MANAGED DEER QUOTA HUNT.*

Directions: *From I-64, take exit 123 and drive 6.6 miles east on US 60 to Salt Lick. Then drive south 3.6 miles on KY 211 to Forest Service Road (FSR) 129. Follow FSR 129 4 miles to FSR 918, then go 9 miles on FSR 918 to area. From I-64, signs lead to campground.*

Ownership: USDA Forest Service (606) 784-6428
Size: 355 acres   **Closest Town:** Salt Lick

Kentucky's four venomous snakes—the copperhead, western cottonmouth, western pygmy rattlesnake, and timber rattlesnake— are pit vipers, named for a conspicuous sensory pit on each side of the head. All have eyes with vertical pupils and bodies that tends to be short and stocky. Some harmless snakes are short and stocky, too, such as the hognose and some water snakes, but their pupils are round.

Description: Surrounded by beautiful Cave Run Lake in an oak-hickory forest, this campground has much to offer visitors. White-tailed deer, gray squirrel, and Canada goose are common year-round and most warbler species use the area, including the ovenbird and yellow warbler. Groundhog, skunk, and opossum also live here. A variety of gull species may be seen in spring, fall, and winter, including ring-billed.

Viewing Information: Best viewing for deer, geese, and squirrels is during winter and early spring. From paved roads, look for deer in mowed fields, mornings and evenings. Does with fawns may be seen June-September. In spring, watch for reptiles and amphibians in woodland pond near amphitheater. Campground contains miles of hiking trails and paved loop roads. In the off-season the campground is closed to motor vehicles and it becomes a delightful place to hike or bike. Trail along lakeshore allows viewing of wintering bald eagles, while another reaches up a mountain to an observation platform. Visitor center on KY 801 (2.3 miles south of US 60) offers information on local wildlife viewing areas and species checklists. Wildlife/music/historical programs, Memorial Day through Labor Day. Special events include a pioneer life day, archeological dig. Platforms, towers; guided/self-guided tours; interpretive center; RV parking; electric hookups; showers; boat rental; swimming beach with bath house. Small entry fee charged per vehicle, half price with Golden Age pass.

Directions: *From I-64, exit south on KY 801 and drive south 3.1 miles to US 60. Turn west on US 60 for 0.2 miles to rejoin KY 801. Continue south 5.8 miles on KY 801 to entrance with large sign.*

Ownership: USDA Forest Service (606) 784-6428
Size: 700 acres   **Closest Town:** Morehead

Kentucky's first bald eagle nest since the 1940s was established in 1985. Later destroyed by storm, the nest on Ballard WMA was 6 feet wide, 4 feet deep, and perched 90 feet up a cypress tree. First-time nesters are usually unsuccessful—but annual returns to the same nest eventually pay off.
GARY CRANDALL

EASTERN

54. SHALLOW FLATS OBSERVATION AREA

Description: This fenced site contains 5 wetlands and 6 acres of meadow on the shores of Cave Run Lake. The site hosts Canada geese year-round. Also look for wood duck, green and great blue heron, and eastern bluebird.

Viewing Information: Only 14 minutes from I-64, this barrier-free site offers year-round viewing of Canada geese. Choose May, June, and July for up-close views of goslings. Winter is best for mallard, black and ring-necked duck, bufflehead, and blue-winged teal; osprey and bald eagle are present in winter and spring. Visitor center and camping nearby. Public invited to help biologists band Canada geese third week of June each year.

Directions: From I-64, drive south 3 miles on KY 801 to US 60. Turn west onto US 60 for 0.2 mile to rejoin KY 801. Drive south 5.3 miles on KY 801 to site. Entrance marked by sign.

Ownership: USDA Forest Service (606) 784-6428
Size: 10 acres   **Closest Town:** Morehead

55. MINOR CLARK FISH HATCHERY

Description: Situated in the Knobs near Cave Run Lake, the hatchery features an oxbow lake, 111 rearing/brood ponds, and hosts numerous wildlife species. Striped bass, hybrid striped bass, largemouth and smallmouth bass, muskellunge, walleye, fathead minnows, and goldfish are all reared annually here. An outdoor display pool filled with a variety of warmwater fish.

Viewing Information: This place is for the birds—viewing them, that is. Look for Canada goose, wood duck, mallard, crane, cattle egret, and black-crowned night heron year-round. In spring and fall look for osprey, plover, sandpiper, killdeer, avocet, stilt, yellowlegs, dunlin, and snipe. Fall sometimes brings cormorant, grebe, and common loon. Ring-billed gull and Caspian tern are common in winter. See snapping and painted turtle inside hatchery Monday through Friday, 7 a.m. to 3 p.m. Barrier-free access to display pool near paved parking area, open April 1 to September 15. Several ponds open year-round, access by gravel roads. Guided tours by appointment.

Directions: From I-64 near Morehead, take exit 133 and travel KY 801 south for 3.2 miles to US 60. Travel west on US 60 for 0.1 mile to KY 801 and turn south, continuing 1.5 miles to hatchery.

Ownership: Kentucky Department of Fish and Wildlife
Resources (606) 784-1176, or (606) 784-6872
Size: 300 acres   **Closest Town:** Morehead

Description: This picturesque area, with its 1,500-acre lake, is known for scenic vertical cliffs and waterfalls towering 150 feet above the lake. The area holds white-tailed deer, gray and fox squirrel, red and gray fox, eastern cottontail rabbit, chipmunk, raccoon, striped skunk, Canada goose, mallard, Cooper's hawk, barred and screech owl, and turkey vulture. Hemlock, holly, rhododendron, ferns (Christmas, New York, walking), and a multitude of wildflowers are common here.

Viewing Information: Primary viewing area is below dam from paved roads. Best viewing is along the self-guided nature trail and an oxbow from old river channel area that contain wildlife/nature study stations. This National Registered Trail follows the Little Sandy River, stocked monthly with rainbow trout and lined with box elders and jewelweed. Quiet observers may glimpse deer traveling the many game paths from food plots to the river or squirrels scampering through tree canopies. Further upland are twisted rock formations where rhododendron and hemlock cling to cliffs overlooking river. Bridges lead across waterfalls where delicate wildflowers decorate the banks. Look for beaver cuttings near the river and squirrel dens and hawk nests high in hardwoods. Near wet areas look for box and painted turtle, various water snakes, salamanders, 5-lined skink, American toad, and bull and leopard frog. In summer look for butterflies, notably the admiral monarch, sulphur, and swallowtails (giant, tiger, spicebush, black). Hawthorn-sumac thickets host hundreds of songbird species: purple finch, eastern flycatcher, wood peewee, eastern meadowlark, purple martin, black-capped chickadee, cedar waxwing, wrens, vireos, red-wing blackbird, mockingbird, cardinal, blue jay, evening grosbeak, and dark-eyed junco, among others. Kentucky's sixth-ever sighting of a scissor-tailed flycatcher occurred here in 1992. Bald eagle seen occasionally. Secluded benches; guided tours upon request; interpretive center; picnic shelters; marina; barrier-free fishing pier.

Directions: Take I-64 to Grayson and follow KY 7 south 8 miles to Grayson Dam.

Ownership: U.S. Army Corps of Engineers (606) 474-5815
Size: 17,000 acres   **Closest Town:** Grayson

Artificial nest boxes are helping eastern bluebirds rebound from widespread pesticide use and the elimination of cavity trees and wooden fence posts. Nest boxes should be placed 4-6 feet above ground in fencerows adjacent to open woodlands, pastures, and farmlands.

EASTERN

EASTERN KENTUCKY

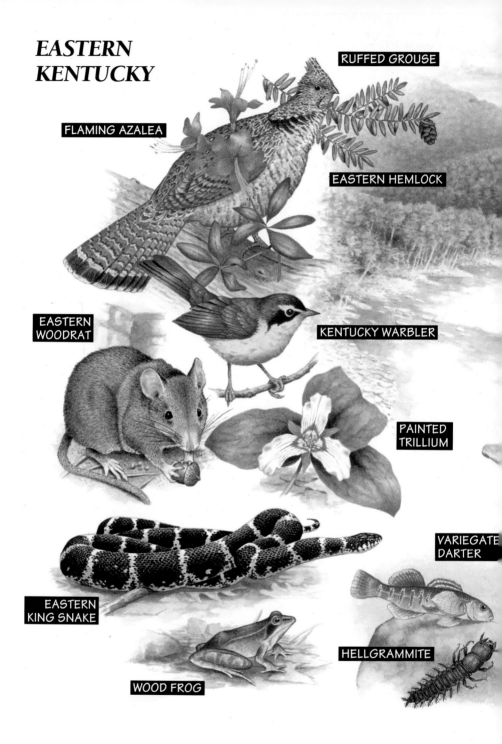

RUFFED GROUSE

FLAMING AZALEA

EASTERN HEMLOCK

EASTERN WOODRAT

KENTUCKY WARBLER

PAINTED TRILLIUM

VARIEGATE DARTER

EASTERN KING SNAKE

HELLGRAMMITE

WOOD FROG

Eastern Kentucky's hills and mountains maintain one of the most diverse forest systems in the nation. It is here the rich "mixed mesophytic forest" is centered. This forest has more tree species growing together in associated plant communities than any other forest type. It naturally follows that this rich forest system is home to a diverse wildlife community.

TULIP-POPLAR

SCARLET TANAGER

LARGE LEAF
MAGNOLIA

BLACK BEAR

PINK LADY'S
SLIPPER

SPOTTED
SALAMANDER

MUSKELLUNGE

GOLDEN REDHORSE

Eastern hills also host the headwaters of numerous rivers and creeks. Forested watersheds provide some of the cleanest water available. These free-flowing waters are home to a multitude of aquatic plants and animals.

Description: More than 20 caverns (some uncharted and home to federally-listed endangered Indiana bats) wind their way beneath rugged upland oak-hickory and mixed pine-hardwood forests. Raccoon, striped skunk, chipmunk, squirrel, eastern cottontail rabbit, opossum, white-tailed deer, red and gray fox, and weasel live here. A 40-acre reservoir, small pond, and freshwater marsh provide inviting habitat for beaver, muskrat, river otter, mink, wood duck, merganser, mallard, grebe, coot, great blue and green heron, and killdeer.

Viewing Information: Forest bird species include red-tailed, broad-wing, and red-shouldered hawk, turkey vulture, great horned, barred, and screech owls, ruffed grouse, woodcock, pileated and red-headed woodpecker, warblers, and other songbirds. Cave tours; guided/self-guided tours on 6 miles of trails; backcountry trail; interpretive center; guided canoe trips on Tygart's Creek.

Directions: *From I-64, take exit 161 to US 60. Travel east 1.4 miles on US 60 and turn north on KY 182. Drive 2.8 miles to park entrance.*

Ownership: Kentucky Department of Parks (606) 286-4411
Size: 1,350 acres   **Closest Town:** Olive Hill

Most active on mornings after a night rain, the eastern box turtle is the only known agent for dispersing Mayapple seeds. A dome shell and unique hinged plastron (undershell) allow this turtle to completely hide its head. Males have red eyes and a concave plastron. The undershell in females is convex and eyes are brown. Life span is 50-75 years; some individuals exceed 100 years of age. GENE BOAZ

58. GREENBO LAKE STATE RESORT PARK

Description: Oak-hickory and mixed pine-hardwood forests harbor large herds of white-tailed deer and also raccoon, red fox, and squirrel. Watch for eastern bluebird, downy woodpecker, wrens, and warblers, including Kentucky. Trout, bass, and catfish thrive in 225-acre Greenbo Lake.

Viewing Information: Best viewing for deer, fox, and birds is along 2 miles of entrance road to lodge. Watch for copperhead and black snake spring through fall. Raccoon, skunk, mallard, geese, red-tailed hawk, and barred owl are common year-round. Guided/self-guided tours; 9 miles of trails; picnic shelters.

Directions: From I-64 at Grayson, drive north 15 miles on KY 1 to park entrance.

Ownership: Kentucky Department of Parks (606) 473-7324
Size: 3,300 acres   **Closest Town:** Greenup

59. JESSE STUART STATE NATURE PRESERVE

Description: This site stretches from ridgetops to the valley along W-Hollow Road. A quarter of the area is pasture; the remainder is maturing second-growth oak-hickory forest with young tulip poplar-maple groves in ravines. Watch for white-tailed deer, wild turkey, rufus-sided towhee, white-eyed vireo, red-tailed hawk, opossum, groundhog, striped skunk, raccoon, gray and fox squirrel, red fox, eastern cottontail rabbit, and chipmunk.

Viewing Information: View mammals and songbirds in spring and fall from 4.5 miles of trails. Nocturnal flying squirrels are common along Shingle Mill and Coon Den Hollow trails. Look for deer in pastures along W-Hollow Road. Walk through wooded valleys in spring to see iris, toothwort, wild geranium, Jack-in-the-pulpit, and wild ginger. Summer brings Joe Pye weed, Mayapple, heal all, golden ragwort, and asters.

Directions: From I-64 at Grayson drive 21.5 miles north on KY 1 and turn left onto W-Hollow Road. Drive 1.6 miles to parking area on right. CAUTION: VERY SHARP CURVES ON W-HOLLOW ROAD.

Ownership: Kentucky State Nature Preserve Commission (502) 573-2886
Size: 733 acres   **Closest Town:** Greenup

Description: Within this 16,000-acre WMA, a special viewing area is set aside on a 1-acre bluff overlooking three 1-acre wetlands managed for waterfowl. Each impoundment is managed differently to provide a variety of habitat conditions, complemented by nearby Cherokee Creek. Wood duck, mallard, black duck, and bufflehead are common; other migratory ducks on the Mississippi Flyway also stop over. Swallows, belted kingfisher, and great blue and green heron use the impoundments, as do beaver, mink, and other freshwater mammals. A wildflower plot next to the parking lot provides habitat for hummingbirds, butterflies, American goldfinch, and other songbirds.

Viewing Information: Best waterfowl viewing is November-March. Look for wood duck spring through fall; teal and bufflehead in September-early October. Migratory shorebirds are present September-November and again in spring. Belted kingfisher, swallows, and heron may be seen throughout summer. Wildflowers reach peak brilliance in late June. WMA also includes upland hardwoods, fields, and 2,242-acre lake with additional viewing opportunities. Self-guided tours; guided tours by appointment.

Directions: *From Blaine, drive 8 miles north on KY 201 to site, marked by signs. CAUTION: KY 201 IS NARROW AND WINDING BUT PASSABLE BY BUSES AND RVs.*

Ownership: U.S. Army Corps of Engineers; managed by Kentucky Department of Fish and Wildlife Resources (502) 564-4406

Size: 4 acres   **Closest Town:** Blaine

Thanks to restoration efforts in Kentucky, white-tailed deer now number in excess of 450,000. Usually arriving as twins, June fawns are sometimes mistaken for orphans by uninformed, would-be rescuers; in most cases, however, well-camouflaged offspring are left alone for long periods while does feed and rest. Wildlife viewers who suspect an animal is orphaned should always leave it undisturbed and contact a conservation officer. GARRY WALTER

Description: On 1,139-acre Paintsville Lake, this site is known for its white-tailed deer and small mammals such as squirrel and eastern cottontail rabbit. Primarily forested in hemlock, oak- hickory, and pines where ruffed grouse, bobwhite, and wild turkey live, the WMA also holds 26 ponds and both warm- and cool-water streams.

Viewing Information: The primary viewing site is the 1.2-mile drive along KY 2275 from entrance to lake, visitor center, and across dam. Area around visitor center offers excellent year-round close-ups of squirrels and a variety of birds, including red-bellied woodpecker and white-breasted nuthatch. Kiwanis Trail, a 1.25-mile walk on the National Register, offers excellent chances to view white-tailed deer as it winds above the lakeshore and loops to the visitor center. Also watch for osprey, wood duck, common loon, and Canada goose. Spring and summer are perfect for viewing a variety of migratory songbirds such as eastern bluebird, blue jay, and American goldfinch. Pileated woodpecker, great blue heron, coot, gulls, and vultures are fairly common year-round. Notable spring wildflowers are Mayapple, bluet, Jack-in-the-pulpit, and crested dwarf iris. In summer look for goldenrod and yellow trout lily. Viewing information and exhibits at visitor center. Guided tours by appointment. Marina with restaurant; picnic shelters; barrier-free fishing pier; trailer parking on gravel shoulder of KY 2275 within 0.5 mile of visitor center. *CAUTION: SOME ROADS ARE UNPAVED AND CAN BECOME SLICK AND HAZARDOUS DURING WINTER. SOME AREAS MAY BE CLOSED DUE TO HIGH WATER.* Call numbers listed below for lake, weather, and road conditions.

Directions: *From Paintsville, drive 0.5 mile west on US 460 to KY 40. Drive 1.6 miles west on KY 40, then 0.8 mile west on KY 2275 to dam. Cross dam and continue 0.5 mile to visitor center.*

Ownership: U.S. Army Corp of Engineers (606) 297-6312; Kentucky Department of Parks (606) 297-4111
Size: 13,093 acres   **Closest Town:** Paintsville

They came for the sake of salt. Grassland buffalo repeatedly traveling the easiest routes to salt licks and water soon left distinct paths later used by Native Americans. Several Kentucky highways were once buffalo trails.

EASTERN

62. LITTCARR WILDLIFE VIEWING AREA

Description: Littcarr Dam not only improves water quality but has created a marsh, an unusual habitat in these mountains. Cattail, bulrush, black willow, sycamore, and birch are home to wood duck, belted kingfisher, great blue and green heron, ruffed grouse, bobwhite, wild turkey, red-winged blackbird, warblers, raccoon, and striped skunk.

Viewing Information: Best viewing is in summer and fall. Kingfisher, grouse, quail, turkey, and blackbird are common year-round. Look for warblers, herons, red-tailed hawk, wood duck, and teal in summer; winter is best for mallard and osprey. Spring and summer blooms include red clover, milkweed, swamp rose mallow, Queen Anne's lace, redbud, and chicory. Viewing is good from KY 15 and KY 160. *CAUTION: HEAVY COAL TRUCK TRAFFIC.* View also from access road to basin. Small gravel parking lot on KY 160; canoe access. Camping nearby.

Directions: From Hindman, drive 14 miles south on KY 160, then 2 miles west on KY 15 to dam.

Ownership: U.S. Army Corps of Engineers (606) 642-3308
Size: 15 acres   **Closest Town:** Hindman

63. LILLEY CORNETT WOODS

Description: This mosaic of virgin forest (250 acres), second-growth forest, and bottomland reverting to woodland boasts both cool- and warm-water streams. Look for bobwhite, ruffed grouse, wild turkey, woodcock, wood duck, common egret, red-shouldered hawk, cardinal, scarlet tanager, eastern bluebird, and hooded and cerulean warbler. Raccoon, beaver, muskrat, river otter, white-tailed deer, and red and gray fox also live here. Wildflowers include pink lady's slipper, trillium, Jack-in-the-pulpit, and trout lily.

Viewing Information: Public access by guided tour on designated trails. Wildlife often seen along 1.5-mile gravel road. Excellent viewing on 6 miles of trails. Visitor center.

Directions: From Hazard, drive 6 miles south on KY 15. Turn right onto KY 7 for 13.9 miles, then right on KY 1103 for 7.6 miles to site.

Ownership: Eastern Kentucky University (606) 622-1476
Size: 554 acres   **Closest Town:** Hazard

Description: Resting atop 2,700-foot Pine Mountain and nestled between the two most southeastern patches of Daniel Boone National Forest, this state park offers spectacular rock outcroppings. Typical upland forest with oak, hickory, pine, beech, birch, and striped maple contains scenic overlooks where ravens soar. Mountain laurel and rhododendron prevail and a few areas hold the rare Frazier magnolia. Black bear are returning to this site. Pileated woodpecker, wild turkey, ruffed grouse, red and gray fox, striped skunk, raccoon, whip-poor-will, black-throated green and Kentucky warbler, and great horned owl may also be seen.

Viewing Information: Wild and domestic waterfowl are seen year-round on 3-acre public fishing lake, home to bass, bluegill, catfish, and rainbow trout. Warm evenings are best for viewing big brown and little brown bat. King and garter snake, timber rattlesnake, and copperhead are relatively common in region. Park map/brochure; picnic shelter; paddle boats.

Directions: *From Harlan, drive 22 miles east on US 119 to park entrance. CAU-TION: ROAD IS PAVED BUT VERY MOUNTAINOUS, STEEP, AND NARROW; MOST HAZARDOUS IN WINTER, WET WEATHER.*

Ownership: Kentucky Department of Parks (606) 589-2479
Size: 1,283 acres   **Closest Town:** Cumberland

Carolina wrens build nests in tree or stump cavities in woodlands with brushy cover. Nests may be constructed 10 feet up, on the ground, or anywhere in between. These birds also readily use nest boxes placed in rural and suburban settings.
JEFFREY A. BROWN

EASTERN

65. LITTLE SHEPHERD TRAIL

Description: Little Shepherd Trail, a rugged, unimproved road, runs along the crest of Pine Mountain between Whitesburg and Harlan. Various species may be observed from the road such as white-tailed deer, wild turkey, ruffed grouse, numerous songbirds, reptiles, amphibians, and, on an increasing frequency, black bear. Plant species are plentiful and include the spectacular catawba rhododendron, yellow fringed orchid, yellow lady's slipper, and Cumberland azalea. Because forested Pine Mountain is higher than the adjacent Cumberland Plateau, views are spectacular, especially during the October foliage display.

Viewing Information: Summer skies, where black and turkey vulture soar, also bring hawks into view such as the red-tailed, red-shouldered, and Cooper's, and American kestrel. Watch for raven, wood thrush, tanager, red-bellied woodpecker, and black-throated green warbler. Bats are plentiful as are pygmy and smoky shrew and golden mouse. The area also holds timber rattlesnake, copperhead, black mountain dusky salamander, and mountain chorus and gray tree frog. Look for yellow lady's slipper in spring; catawba, mid to late May; mountain laurel and Cumberland azalea, late May to early June; yellow fringed orchid and rosebay rhododendron, summer; showy gentian, fall. Hemlock cove forests and many small bogs are within walking distance of trail. Facilities and recreation available at Kingdom Come State Park (see Site 64).

Directions: *From McDonald's restaurant in Whitesburg, take KY 119 south 4.6 miles to crest of Pine Mountain; continue on KY 119 for 0.5 mile to beginning of Little Shepherd Trail on right. Pine Mountain WMA sign at turn. Trail runs 11 miles southwest to Kingdom Come State Park. (NOTE: This is the main trail section. Travelers wishing to view other portions should get directions from local residents.) CAUTION: UNIMPROVED ROAD. During dry conditions a pickup truck with positive traction and snow/mud tires will suffice. 4x4 vehicles work well except during extreme conditions such as heavy snow. Pull vehicle completely off road when stopping.*

Ownership: Harlan and Letcher County Fiscal Courts; contact Kingdom Come State Park (606) 589-2479
Size: 11 miles   **Closest Town:** Whitesburg

66. HENSLEY SETTLEMENT, CUMBERLAND GAP NATIONAL HISTORIC PARK

Description: Situated on an isolated plateau astride Brush Mountain, Hensley Settlement is a remnant community of 12 scattered farmsteads. The settlement was established in 1904. With its split-rail fences and buildings of hewn chestnut logs and shake roofs, Hensley Settlement flourished nearly 5 decades. After 1965, the National Park Service restored some of the farmsteads and the schoolhouse and cemetery. Restored buildings and fields are maintained by farmer-demonstrators using many techniques employed by earlier dwellers.

Viewing Information: White-tailed deer and wild turkey live on the plateau, along with Kentucky warbler and wood frog. Evenings during spring and fall, deer visit open fields. Visitors may also view wildlife by walking gravel service road. Brush Mountain holds the headwaters of a brook trout stream. Park contains 50 miles of hiking trails; 5 primitive campgrounds in backcountry, accessible by foot only. Permit required for overnight. A 160-site campground is located across the state line on US 58 in Virginia. *CAUTION: NEVER HIKE ALONE IN THIS WILD AREA. AVOID VISITING DURING DEER GUN HUNTING SEASONS.* Daily interpretive programs mid-June through Labor Day and weekends, spring and fall.

Directions: *Take US 25 east to Middlesboro and Cumberland Gap National Historic Park. From the park visitor center, Hensley Settlement can be reached by foot trail or 4x4 vehicle in dry weather. CAUTION: ACCESS TO SETTLEMENT IS RUGGED AND STEEP.*

Ownership: National Park Service (606) 248-2817
Size: 100 acres   **Closest Town:** Middlesboro

Living in woodlands near temporary ponds, spotted salamanders may hide under leaf litter, rocks, or boards during warm months. Graceful underwater dances on pond bottoms highlight the early spring mating rituals of these amphibians. GENE BOAZ

Where The Wild Things Are

Falcon Press puts wildlife viewing secrets at your fingertips with our high-quality, full color guidebooks—the Watchable Wildlife Series. This is the only official series of guides for the National Watchable Wildlife Program: areas featured in the books correspond to official sites across America. And you'll find more than just wildlife. Many sites boast beautiful scenery, interpretive displays, opportunities for hiking, picnics, biking, plus—a little peace and quiet. So pick up one of our Wildlife Viewing Guides today and get close to Mother Nature!

Watch This Partnership Work

The National Watchable Wildlife Program was formed with one goal in mind: get people actively involved in wildlife appreciation and conservation. Defenders of Wildlife has led the way by coordinating this unique multi-agency program and developing a national network of prime wildlife viewing areas.

Part of the proceeds go to conserve wildlife and wildlife habitat.

Visit your local bookstore for more information or call toll-free for a free catalog of nature-related books and gift ideas.

1-800-582-2665
Falcon Press
P.O. Box 1718
Helena, MT 59624